Developing Economies of the Third World

Outstanding Studies of Economic Development in Latin America and the Pacific Rim

EDITED BY
Stuart Bruchey

A Garland Series

THE EFFICIENCY OF
THE MEXICAN
STOCK MARKET

MIGUEL HAKIM

GARLAND PUBLISHING, INC.
NEW YORK & LONDON
1992

LIBRARY OF CONGRESS CATALOGING-IN-PUBLICATION DATA

Hakim, Miguel.
The efficiency of the Mexican stock market / Miguel Hakim.
p. cm. — (Developing economies of the Third World)
Originally published as the author's thesis (Ph. D., Claremont
University, 1988)
Includes bibliographical references.
ISBN 0-8153-0628-8 (alk. paper)
1. Stock-exchange—Mexico. 2. Efficient market theory.
I. Title. II. Series.
HG5162.H35 1992

332.64'272—dc20   91-44141

Designed by Lisa Broderick

Printed on acid-free, 250-year-life paper.
MANUFACTURED IN THE UNITED STATES OF AMERICA

THE EFFICIENCY OF THE MEXICAN STOCK MARKET

ACKNOWLEDGEMENTS

I sincerely want to thank the members of my dissertation's committe, Professors Richard J. Sweeney, Jerome B. Baesel, Thomas D. Willett, James P. Giles, and John B. Rae for their guidance and encouragement in accomplishing the task of writing this work.

I am most grateful to Professor Sweeney for the training he has provided. His impact on the formation of my personal goals in the field of finance will be influential for many years to come.

Honor is also extended to Professor Baesel for making substantive comments regarding normality tests as well as on my work on international diversification.

The route to this book was certainly a challenging one and at times seemed endless. However, many obstacles were overcome with the support of my parents, Ivonne and Felipe, and my everlasting companion, Martha. Special thanks go to my colleagues Patchara Surajaras and Mark Bremer who assisted me with computer work and provided valuable feedback on my work.

Part of the early research was funded by the University of the Americas in Cholula, Mexico. I would like to express my gratitude to Luis A. Casas in Operadora de Bolsa who was flexible enough to let me finish the last part of this work.

Finally, I would like to extend thanks to all those people without whose labor, time and assistance this book would never have been completed.

TABLE OF CONTENTS

LIST OF CHARTS

LIST OF TABLES

CHAPTER I

INTRODUCTION

The finance literature abounds with applications of efficiency tests for American stock data[1]. There is a lack of corresponding studies for Mexican securities, due primarily to the absence of generally available computer readable data bases. One of the main objectives of this work is to expand the entries of a file originally developed by the Instituto Tecnológico Autónomo de México (I.T.A.M.), containing weekly and monthly adjusted prices on 91 stocks for the 1972-1981 period, in order to perform test of efficiency of the Mexican stock market.

Although the data base is not updated until 1991, this book tells the reader most of what he or she wants to know regarding the current organization and trading mechanism of the Mexican stock market. This is important considering the difficulty in finding a coherent and comprehensive work on the subject written even in the Spanish language[2].

This study is organized as follows. Chapter II analyzes the current structure of the Mexican stock market. It includes some descriptive statistics on the supply and demand of shares as well as the intermediaries. Chapter III describes the data, the performance of some tests on the type of distributions of returns, and it shows the effects of domestic as well as international diversification. Chapter IV presents the empirical results on serial correlation tests and filter rules on both returns and excess returns. Corrections for thin trading were executed in determinig the expected returns of stocks and portfolios. Chapter V displays the conclusions.

To reduce the burden of going through this rather lengthy investigation, a brief summary of each chapter is presented below.

Chapter II describes how the period of institutionalization began in 1975 with the issuance of the securities market law in which the National Securities Commission was given power to regulate the market. The three regional exchanges at the time merged a year latter, and formed the only exchange

---

[1] For a well-known review article see : E. F. Fama, "Efficient Capital Markets: A Review of Theory and Empirical Work", Journal of Finance, (May 1970) : 383-417.

[2] Most of the information is scattered in pamphlets, bulletins and internal operational rules of the Mexican stock exchange. The National Securities Commission also publishes rules to regulate new events.

operating in Mexico at the present time, Bolsa Mexicana de Valores S.A. de C.V. Since then, brokers can only be organized as corporations.

Investors willing to buy or sell stocks listed in the exchange must operate through a broker who has representatives on the floor of the exchange. Investors specify to the broker the type of transaction (spot, forward or future), and the conditions under which a stock is going to be bought or sold (market, limit or contingent orders).

Once the broker has received instructions, the order is transmitted to its representative on the floor of the exchange. Here, stocks are designated to a specific location and broker's representatives go to that station to post, shout out (personal) or cross orders. There is no specialist or assigned market-maker. This causes that transactions for some stocks are not very frequent (thin trading) and that their price may change substantially. This is why the exchange in order to avoid excessive and erratic price changes uses a limit of fluctuation which is equal to last transaction's price, plus or minus 5%. If a transaction goes beyond the current limit, it will be suspended for 60 and 90 minutes, the first and second time, respectively.

When the order is executed, the broker is entitled to a fixed commission. This means, a fixed rate for all customers of a given size regardless of which member firm handles the order. There is a cheaper commission for commercial banks and brokerage houses buying or selling for their own account, and even a cheaper one for mutual funds. 88.5 % of the total commission is kept by the member firm executing the order. The rest is distributed among the contingency fund in favor of investors, the exchange, the Mexican Association of Brokerage Houses, and the Institute for the Stock Deposit.

The system of fixed commissions has put small member firms in an unfavorable position due to the fact that they can not offer the same kind of services that the big ones do, such as security analysis, quotation boards, research reports, etc.. The author proposes a change from fixed to flexible commissions in the Mexican stock exchange. This will allow firms to tailor prices to the services offered. The investors will be better off by having lower transaction costs and a wider range of options.

There are many of the 500 biggest Mexican corporations in terms of sales that are yet no listed in the exchange. This can be partially explanied by such factors such as the fiscal policy which until 1986 permitted corporations to deduct interest payments causing a bias against equity financing, and the group or family structure prevailing in the Mexican industry. When corporations finally decide to go public, the group controls most of the shares a only a few percentage is freely traded.

Chapter II finishes discussing the evolution of the stock index published by the exchange. The behavior of the market as measured by the index was practically stagnant from 1970 until the last part of 1977. There was a boom from 1977 until the first quarter of 1979. The decline came in the last part of

1979 and continued until 1982. The beginning of a new bullish environment happened in 1983 and lasted until the first part of 1986, date in which a superboom started and reached its highest point in October of 1987. The crash came in only three months with a decrease of 77% in the index.

Chapter III describes the data used in this work. The data file includes simple rate of returns on stocks which are calculated adjusting closing prices for cash and stock dividends, subscriptions, and splits. It also contains: returns on a market value index, returns on randomly selected portfolios, returns on a risk-free asset, information concerning trading frequencies, the inflation rate, the exchange rate between the Mexican peso and the American dollar, and returns on some American stocks and indexes.

The old stock price index published by the exchange was based on a fixed sample of 29 stocks. It did not adjust for subscriptions. The index was in operation until September of 1980. It was modified because the fixed sample was not representative of the listed stocks at the end of the 70's. Furthermore, it was necessary to improve the relative weight of each stock because the old index accounted for price, but not for the number of shares outstanding. The new index uses a dynamic sample of stocks that is revised every other month and it weights stocks using both price and shares outstanding. The sample for July-August of 1991 consists of 40 stocks. The stocks in the sample are those having higher liquidity, higher percentage held by the public, and price variability similar to the variability of the market.

Statistics regarding the distributions of returns on common stocks are presented [3]. The first two moments of the distribution (mean and standard deviation) are calculated on simple returns whereas the third and fourth moments (skewness and kurtosis) are calculated on continously compounded returns.

On average, the mean and standard deviation of both weekly and monthly returns on stocks and portfolios, are lower in the 1972-1976 period than in the 1977-1981 period. However, in both subperiods the average mean return on stocks is greater than the average inflation rate, yielding investors positive real returns.

The symmetry of the distribution, as measured by the skewness coefficient, indicates that individual stock and portfolio returns are skewed to the right. Skewness can stem from extreme observations or discrete-jump processes. Another possible explanation for positive skewness is that investors usually do not lose more than 100%, whereas capital gains are unlimited[4].However, this

---

[3] Return and rate of return are used interchangeably.

[4] An investor can lose more than 100% on margin accounts and by short selling.

asymmetry dissapears when one claculates the skewness coefficient on monthly individual stocks and portfolios.

The peakness of the distribution, as measured by the kurtosis, indicates that stock and portfolio returns are more peaked than normal distributions. This result is the same for both weekly and monthly returns. In addition, studentized range tests on countinously compounded returns reject the normality hypothesis in favor of the hypothesis that the weekly and monthly samples come from a distribution that is "fat-tailed" relative to a normal.

Chapter III also looks at domestic as well as international diversification. One could distinguish between price changes which can be attributed to the market as a whole, called systematic risk; and those which are independent of general market fluctuations, called unsystematic risk. The latter can be reduced by diversification within the stock market. Up to a point, the spreading of funds over a number of stocks will reduce risk more than proportionately to the reduction in return. This is based on the fact that the correlation among stocks is not perfect. Almost all unsystematic risk in the Mexican stock market is eliminated by holding a randomly selected portfolio of 16-20 stocks. There is additional reduction of risk by holding a portfolio containing both Mexican and American securities. The advantages of an extended or international diversification can be seen by comparing the average correlation coefficient on Mexican equities (0.24) with the average correlation coefficient of a portfolio formed with Mexican and American stocks (0.17).

Tests of efficiency are presented in Chapter IV. Serial correlation tests on stock returns display a preponderance of significant negative coefficients. This significance is quite consistent over time. In contrast, tests on portfolio returns show some significant positive coefficients. The results seem to indicate some linear dependencies during the period of time analyzed. Similar results are obtained when autocorrelation tests are applied to real returns calculated by substracting the inflation rate from the nominal returns.

The serial correlation tests do not include risk in the analysis. The construction of general equilibrium models allows the determination of the relevant measure of risk and the relationship between expected returns and risk for any asset when markets are in equilibrium. What constitutes risk and how it should be measured, is still a point of controversy.

The Market Model and the Capital Asset Pricing Model (C.A.P.M.) are used to introduce risk in the analysis and to determine expected returns. The measure of risk (beta) was corrected for negative serial correlation and heteroscedasticity.

Because reported closing prices typically represent trades prior to the actual close of the trading day, measured returns very often deviate from true returns. This anomaly in the way the data is collected introduces into the Market Model or any other model using beta, the econometric problem of errors-in variable which in turn causes Ordinary Least Squares estimators to be biased and inconsistent. This problem is more severe, the shorter the interval used to estimate returns.

In the Mexican stock exchange, we find that many listed shares are traded infrequently. That is why the beta was also adjusted for thin trading using the procedures developed by Scholes and Williams (1977), Dimson (1979), and Fowler and Rorke (1983). They present analytical as well as empirical evidence that betas that trade less (more) frequently that the index used in their estimation are downward (upward) biased. This work presents evidence showing that the Market Model or the C.A.P.M. beta is increaŝed by nearly 90% in most cases when estimation procedures that take into consideration trading frequencies are applied. The results are mixed when stocks that trade very frequently are utilized. A possible explanation is that the most heavily weighted stocks in the old market index are moderate trading stocks.

It is also important for investment analysis and forecasting purposes to examine the stationarity of the beta coefficient. The stationarity of beta is checked using a Chow test that shows that betas of portfolios are stable but betas of individual stocks are unstable.

Having found a way to determine the relationship between expected return for any asset or group of assets, serial correlation tests can be applied to excess returns. Excess return is defined here as the difference between actual return and what is expected under the C.A.P.M. The overall results show that the pattern found in returns is even more pronounced when tests are applied to excess returns.

There is an infinite number of possible filter rules on can address, but all of them as well as the methods of technical analysis rest on the assumption that the market repeats itself in patterns. Therefore, one can only test specific filter rules to see if they work. Sweeney (1986), not only provides a risk adjusted rule which is very appropiate for the Mexican stock market, but also develops a statistic which compares the filter's return with a measure of its equilibrium value. Specifically, the rule begins with the investor in the particular stock. If the stock's price falls z percent below its past local high, the investor sells the stock at the closing price and invests the money in the risk-free rate. Then, the investor follows the stock until its price rises y percent above its past local low, at which time funds are taken from the risk-free asset to buy the stock at the closing price. Both normal and reverse filters ranging from 0.5 percent to 50 percent were applied to weekly returns on 34 individual stocks and to an equally-weighted portfolio over the 1972-1981 period. Only in very few cases both normal and reverse filters on individual stocks surpassed a buy-and-hold strategy after minimum commissions are included. Significance before commissions is achieved in three out of the 30 filters reported for an equally-weighted portfolio. However, all the significant profits are eliminated with the inclusion of minimum transaction costs.

CHAPTER II

MARKET STRUCTURE

The market for most Mexican stocks is relatively illiquid. Trading is infrequent, price changes may be large and order executions may be slow. Although it was formally incorporated in the Securities Market Law of 1990; the exchange does not have a specialist system as does the New York Stock Exchange. Under the specialist system each stock traded is assigned a specialist who supervises and conducts a fair and orderly market for that security. To perform their function, specialists are obliged to act in two forms: as agents who buy and sell stock for the accounts of others and as principals who buy and sell for their own account in order to maintain marketability (liquidity to investors) and an ordely succession of prices. The fact that the Mexican stock market does not use specialists does not necessarily mean that the market is not maintained fairly and orderly.

The Mexican batch or periodic call trading system develops in a market in which the brokerage sector is fairly concentrated. Thus, the accumulation of orders give them valuable information to trade for their own account. This is why major member firms frequently trade stocks and fulfill a quasi-specialist function in those issues, but no ongoing market-making responsability is required. That is, there are some brokers acting as dealers implicitly and informally. They buy or sell for their own account with the purpose of making a capital gain, not with the purpose of maintaining a fair and orderly market. To deal with this asymmetric information and in order to avoid big price changes, the exchange uses a 5 % price change limit as a stabilization mechanism, giving the opportunity to equalize the flow of information following a major event.

Instead of the specialist system, stocks are assigned to a specific location on the floor and broker's representatives proceed to that spot to post, shout out or cross orders. This is how public orders are matched.

In March 1991, the National Securities Commission authorized some brokerage houses to conduct short selling procedures on 22 frequently traded stocks. Normally, investors buy stocks before they sell them, and this position is said to be long. However, this process can be reversed using short selling procedures. In a short sale, investors sell stocks they do not own and incur the obligation to buy them back later to cover the short position. This is done by borrowing stocks for use in the initial trade from the brokerage firm's own inventory or from that of another investor. Those who engage in short sales always expect a decline in price. That is, they expect to sell high now and then buy back low. The risk in a short sale is that the market value of the stock will rise and thus force the investor to buy the stock back for a higher price than the sale price. Therefore, one of the problems of not alowing short sales is that investors can only profit in a bull market. The absence of short sales causes a higher volatity in price changes. When investors think the market is "too high", they start to sell short creating an additional supply which in turn helps prevent prices to reach extremely high levels. In a bear market, those who sold short have to buy the securities back. These investors constitute potential buyers representing an additional demand which in turn helps prevent prices to reach extremely low levels. Short selling also causes a higher turnover of the outstanding securities. This helps the liquidity of the system and to solve partially the problem of thin trading. However, the way short selling mechanism is set up in Mexico could make the gap bigger between frequently traded stocks and infrequently traded stocks. Paradoxicaly, this could worse the liquidity of the global stock market.

A. THE STOCK EXCHANGE AS PART OF THE FINANCIAL SYSTEM

Recently, the federal government has decided to rely more upon the private sector and market signals to direct the allocation of resources. This is why commercial banks can determine freely the interest rate on deposits and choose the best option on making loans. The only restriction they face is that a predefined percent of their deposit must be invested in governmental securities.

Starting in July 1990, President Salinas has changed the basic structure of the Mexican Financial System by allowing the private sector participate 100% in commercial banks as well as the possibility of forming financial groups. The concept behind the formation of financial groups is that of "Universal Banking" which refers to the combination of commercial banking (collecting deposits and making loans) and investment banking (issuing, underwriting, placing and trading securities).

Accoridng to the law regulating financial groups, one could be formed by a holding company which owns a minimum of 51% of at least three of the following institutions:
- Commercial Bank
- Brokerage House
- Insurance Company
- Financial Leasing Company
- Currency Exchange House
- Factoring Company
- Bonding Company
- General Warehouse Company
- Investment Company

Foreing investors can participate up to 30% in commercial banks as well as brokerage houses, and up to 49% in insurance companies, general warehouses, factoring, bonding and leasing companies.

Alternatively to the formal constitution of a financial group, a brokerage house which is not part of a group or a commercial bank could own a factoring company, a general warehouse, a leasing company, mutual funds and investment companies. It is necessary to get authorization of the Ministry of Finance to form the parent company with its affiliates or subsidiaries. In this particular scenario, a brokerage house could not own stock of a commercial bank and viceversa.

Adequate regulation and supervision ought to overcome the possible concentration of power among a few institutions and for solving potential conflicts of interest. If this happens the success of universal banking will reflect the economies of scale and scope enjoyed by large and diversified financial institution.

The current structure of the Financial System in its simplest form is presented in charts II.1 and II.2.

The Ministry of Finance and Public Credit, one of the most powerful agencies in the President's cabinet, is still responsible for the financial system. It regulates, controls and supervises the financial operations via the central bank (Banco de México), the National Banking Commission, the National Securities Commission, and the National Insurance and Bonding Commission.

The central bank, established in 1925, has the traditional powers and responsibilities. That is: a) it regulates the issuance and circulation of currency, credit and exchane rates; b) it operates as a reserve bank, and c) it acts as the government's banker, representative and adviser. It is important to note that the central bank is not independent whithin the government but is an instrument of the federal government. The actions of the central bank are subject to the approval of the Ministry of Finance, whose actions are authorized by the President.

The National Banking Commission is the supervisory agency for the technical aspects of bank operations. Mexico's banking law provides for a detailed regulation of many asset and liability categories, and the Commission must interpret, apply and enforce this law.

The National Securities Commission was established in 1946 with the purpose of completing the process by which corporations could sell their stock to the public. In reality, however, it had very little power. It only functioned as a adviser to the Ministry of Finance. The primary responsibility for the stock operation was assigned to the banking Commission and to the principal development bank, Nacional Financiera. In spite of this, the Securities Commission was successful in the approval of institutional investments and the creation of mutual funds.

The Securities Market Law of 1975 marked a turning point for the stock market. That year, the National Securities Commission was made an autonomous institutions. It was given governmental support to supervise all the participants in the stock market and ensure adherance to the rules set up in the law. To be more specific, the Commission now: a) authorizes and controls the issue of new securities, brokers and exhcanges; b) regulates the operation of mutual funds; c) supervises the operation of the Institute for Stock Deposit; d) keeps the national statistics on securities and brokers; and e) acts as a referee in problems between brokers and their clients.

Since the central bank, Nacional Financiera, and the National Banking Commission continually intervene and participate in the securities market, the National Securities Commission must work closely with these institutions. Its decisions often reflect their general aims and policies.

The purpose of this section was to place the stock exchange within the financial system. It was not intended to discuss every sector of chart II.1. Therefore, I shall proceed with some background of the Mexican stock exchange.

B. HISTORY OF THE STOCK EXCHANGE[5]

The stock exchange goes back to 1894 when a group of people in Mexico City decided to start a private institution, Bolsa de Valores de Mexico, to help organize and control buyers and sellers of the very few stocks then traded informally. This was an isolated institution because it was not part of the formal credit system of the time.

The institution suffered many modifications until 1933, year in which it was authorized to serve as an auxiliary organization along with financial corporations (Financieras). The law of credit institutions and auxiliary organizations of 1932 gave these two groups the task of promoting the capital markets. However, the law assigned a more powerful role to the financial corporations than to the Bolsa de Valores de Mexico. In 1940, Nacional Financiera was given very special powers to urge on stock exchanges and financial corporations. Unfortunately, the institution did not respond as expected. The financial corporations stopped being an auxiliary institution in 1941 and they adquired the character of a credit institution.

---

[5] Parts of this section were based on : Jorge Caso B. , "El Mercado de Valores y la Banca: 40 años de Historia". Documentos Mexicanos de Análisis, Instituto de Formación y Desarrollo Profesional de Operadora de Bolsa, México, 1986.

In 1950, the second regional exchange, la Bolsa de Valores de Monterrey, was opened. Seven years later, the third regional exchange, la Bolsa de Valores de Guadalajara, was in operation. Of the three exchanges authorized in the 60's, the one in Mexico City covered approximately 90% of all the transactions.

Up until the last part of the 70's, the banking system (credit institutions) dominated the capital and money markets. They issued long term securities (bonos) and sold them over the counter. In practice, these securities functioned as checking accounts paying interest because the banks guaranteed repurchasing the securities any time at par. The high degree of liquidity within the banks (more deposits than withdrawals) and the confidence of the public on them, made possible this practice until 1976 when the securities disappeared.

From the 50's to the mid-70's, the high productivity of capital gave very good profits to corporations. However, due to deficiencies in the fiscal system, most of the profits ended in the owner's pocket tax free. The owners could not do all this if their corporations were public. Therefore, stockholders had an incentive to keep their corporations private. If there were new projects, corporations borrowed money because the rate of return on investment was greater than the cost of borrowing. In addition, stockholders did not need a secondary market to provide liquidity because they could use their stock as collateral with banks to get all the money they needed. This is why it is possible to say that the stock market was used to finance stockholders not corporations and that it dealt mainly with debts not with equities.

The securities market law of 1975 started the period of institutionalization of the stock market. The law's motive mentioned that the institutional framework is a necessary but not a sufficient condition for the development of the stock market. Before 1975 the legal precepts were scattered over many different laws. The securities market law put them together in one piece and gave them the general framework to foster and regulate not only securities but exchanges and brokers as well. It is important to mention the most relevant aspects of the law:

a) The stock exchanges were not considered auxiliary organizations anymore. They became autonomous institutions having the same category as the banking institutions.

b) The three regional stock exchanges merged in 1976. They formed the only exchange operating in Mexico nowadays, Bolsa Mexicana de Valores S.A. de C.V., based in Mexico City.

c) As it was mentioned before, the National Securities Commission was given special powers to regulate the market. In addition to supervising the adherence to the law by all the participants in the stock market, the Commission has the power to regulate new events through rules. This has the purpose of protecting the public interest by establishing mechanisms to process and publish all the necessary information concerning securities, brokers, transactions, etc.

d) Brokers were given the exclusive power to act as direct intermediaries of securities. Since 1975 they can only be organized as corporations with a minimun equity set up by the Commission[6]. All the brokers who merged to form brokerage houses were given a competitive advantage, since transactions for their own account were made proportional to their equities.

e) With the purpose of unifying markets, all the transactions of securities made by credit institutions must be operated through brokers.

The institutional framework, the devaluation of the peso in 1976 that caused a huge withdrawal of bank deposits, the necessity of the government to finance its public deficit and to create the proper mechanism to deal with open market operations, created a strong money market in 1978 with the issuance for the first time of treasury bills. Furthermore, the high degree of liquidity, the excellent results reported by corporations listed in the exchange, combined with a stronger structure of brokerage houses and more information through the media, caused a boom in the stock market in 1978-1979.

The Institute for the Stock Deposit was created in 1979 as a public entity with the purpose of centralizing the custody and management of securities. This eliminated the impractical and uneconomical physical movements of stock whenever they were exchanged. The new mechanism now tranfers securities through accounting entries.

In 1980, the Mexican Association of Brokerage Houses was established to serve as representative of the group. The same year, the now, Mexican Institute of Capital Markets was created with the purpose of training the personnel of brokerage houses.

The expropiation of the banking system in September of 1982 caused strong changes not only in the stock market but in the financial system as well. This situation opened the possibility for other intermediary sectors to play a more important role. In the particular case of the stock market this opportunity was used to full advantage. The brokerage, insurance and bonding companies owned by banks were returned or sold to the private sector. The government decided to leave to the private sector all those areas that were less developed and promoted within the financial system.

At the end of 1983, privileged information regarding listed stocks in the exchange was regulated. Two years later, the contingency fund in favor of investors in the securities market was institutionalized. This fund was established in 1980 between the exchange and the authorized brokers with the purpose of protecting investors against illicit acts of any brokerage house.

---

[6] The minimum equity requirement to form a brokerage house was 30,000 million pesos in July 1990.

In December of 1986, the Institute for the Stock Deposit stopped being a public entity. The Institute did not change purpose. The state decided to give the ownership and management of the institute to the brokerage houses and kept the licensing of these types of institutes in other cities.

All these events that took place after the expropiation of the banks lead to more autonomy for the stock market. The results of this autonomy can be seen now when the market is raising capital, not debts as it used to be.

C. TYPE OF ORDERS

All the investors willing to buy or sell shares listed in the exchange must operate through a broker that has at least two representatives on the auction floor of the exchange. Brokers will accept three kind of instructions regarding the conditions under which a share is going to be purchased or sold.

a) MARKET ORDER. the investor instructs the broker to buy or sell a stated number of shares at the best available price or prices. This is the most usual procedure.

b) LIMIT ORDER. the investor specifies to the broker not only the number of shares but also the highest price for buying and/or the lowest price for selling. Most of the limit orders are canceled if they are not executed by the end of the day they are placed.

c) CONTINGENT ORDER. the investor instructs the broker to execute a transaction only if something else has been done. For example, a broker might be told to sell a stock at one price and when sold, immediately to buy another. The purpose of the order would be to make sure that funds were available for the the purchase. Another example would be an order to buy 300 shares of FRISCO if its price has dropped to $ 1,900.

D. ORDER SIZES AND TICKS (PRICE INTERVALS)

Every order must specify the number of shares or trading units which are to be bought or sold. Currently, a round lot order may have 500, 1000, 2000, 5000, 10,000, 20,000 or 100,000 units depending on the price of the share. Odd lots are orders containing fewer units than a round lot.

Once the number of shares outstanding is set by the corporation, the price will change on the exchange to reflect supply and demand. However, trading shares in the Mexican exchange takes place at different peso intervals. These intervals (ticks) depend on the price level of the share.

Table II.3 shows the current round lots and price intervals of the Mexican stock exchange. Table II.4 shows how round lots and ticks were calculated in the 1987-1991 period. Finally, Tables II.5 and II.6 present round lots and price intervals prevailing before 1987.

E. TYPE OF TRANSACTIONS

Transactions in the exchange concerning stocks can be classified according to the way they are settled or to the way they are concerted.

Considering the period of time in which transactions are going to be paid, three possiblities arise.

a) SPOT. the payment is made 48 hours after the order is executed. That is, the buyer must pay within two working-days after his or her broker completed the order and the seller must deliver the shares within 48 hours after the order is completed.

b) FORWARD. the two parties decide the day of payment. The only restriction is that the payment can be postpone from 3 to 360 days.

c) FUTURE. the payment is made at preset dates fixed by the exchange. The main differences between forward and future transactions are presented below.

	FORWARD	FUTURE
MATURITY	From 3 to 360 days	The closest Monday to the 10th of each odd month. The parties can choose up to the next three preset dates
TYPE OF SECURITY	Any share listed in the exchange	Only those shares authorized by the exchange
GUARANTEE	The seller must have all the shares to be delivered. The buyer must deposit the difference between the forward price and the base price, plus 5% of the base price	Both the buyer and the seller must deposit 10% of the transaction
SETTLEMENT	a) At maturity b) Before maturity if both parties agree	a) At maturity b) Using reverse operations c) By difference
RIGHTS	They belong to the buyer	Positions are adjusted
PROFIT AND LOSSES	None	They are settled daily

Stock futures were very rare and most of them were used for both individuals and corporations only for fiscal reasons. This is why the exchange decided to suspend them at the end of June of 1987.

Forward transactions, which is also a form a leverage, were heavily used by investors during the boom in the first half of 1987. These transactions, along with margin accounts, caused severe problems to investors and brokers when the market declined drastically in October of the same year. That is why the exchange also suspended these transactions in December of 1987.

The exchange is looking for new ways of operating both forward and futures and it is probable to have them back soon in a revised form.

According to the manner in which orders are operated by the representative of the broker on the auction floor, transactions can be classified in four groups.

a) POST. the representative fills out a form specifying issue, volume, price and time. The form is placed in the corresponding post and registered chronologically. The personnel of the exchange will give priority to the order offering the best price an will use a first in first out procedure to complete transactions having the same price.

These types of orders can be completed by the exchange personnel if the conditions are met or by other representatives going to the pit and saying "CLOSE BUYING" or "CLOSE SELLING" and signing the corresponding form.

The spot order place through posts will always have priority over other kinds of orders if the price of a share coincides. Such orders are also called orders with no restrictions.

b) PERSONAL. instead of filling out forms and place them in the posts, the representative can use his speaking mechanism on the floor to complete orders. He would start saying loudly: "I BUY/SELL 100 SHARES OF TAMSA AT $ 10,000". The representative who wants to accept the proposal will do it answering with the word "CLOSED". Finally, the seller has to fill out a form and report the transactions to the personnel of the exchange.

c) CROSSED. when the representative of a stockbrokerage house has orders from different clients to buy and sell the same share at the same price, he can cross such an order on the floor.

The representative will go to the spot assigned for these transactions where there are judges of the exchange supervising the operation. To announce the transaction, the representative will ring a bell provided with a spring that will turn on a green light. Then, he will say clearly the type of transaction, the share, the volume and the price. If a representative from another stockbrokerage house is interested in the transaction, he would intervene saying "GIVE" or "TAKE" specifying the round lots he is interested in selling or buying. In this particular case, the transaction must be closed with an up-tick in case he takes or with a down-tick in case he gives. Once the crossed order is concluded, the representative has to fill out a form and give it to the judge for final verification and approval.

d) BED. this is an order having no restrictions, with the option to buy or sell a share within a fixed price range. To begin, the representative says loudly the kind of order, the share, the volume and the difference between the prices that are going to be revealed later. Once the order is accepted by another representative, the former must disclose the purchase price and the selling price. Finally, the other representative has to exercise the option of buying or selling at the given prices. These kinds of transactions are very unusual in the exchange.

From this discussion, the reader may have noticed that in the Mexican stock exchange, the word of a broker's representatives is the fundamental principle upon which transactions are made. This is why the exchange has used the latin motto "DICTUM MEUM PACTUM" which means "my word is my contract".

F. THE TRADING FLOOR

The trading floor of the stock exchange is the heart of the Mexican stock market. This is where one individual broker and representatives of 25 brokerage houses get together to execute orders and prices of securities are determined through the process of bidding and offering. Most bids and offers are made by the outside investing public, although a substantial volume of buying and selling is done by members of the exchange.

The floor is divided into six active trading or station posts that are units of service and control through which the process of registering and settling transactions is performed. The six posts make a circle in which exchange clerks work. In addition to the personnel of the exchange, each post counts with computer terminals, as well as monitors. Extending around the circle of the trading floor, there are pits with computer terminals and telephones used to transmit orders from the broker's office to the exchange floor and to report back to the office the execution of such orders. Finally, there is a gallery in which visitors are given the opportunity to watch brokers executing orders and the quotations listed on the blackboards.

Each station is reserved for transactions on specific securities. Post number one is designed for shares of brokerage houses and banks. Stations number two, three and four are reserved for all kind of transactions concerning stocks. The stocks are distributed among these stations in alphabetical order (A-

Cr in post No 2, Co-Na in post No 3 and Ne-Z in post No 4). Post number five is allocated to odd lot-transactions. Post number six is designed to transactions with debentures and government bonds.

The sessions are supervised by personnel of the exchange within the authorized transaction's schedule for capital markets which currently runs from 9:00 to 13:30 hours.

As soon as a transaction is concerted on the floor or as soon as an order is placed through the stations, it will show on the monitors as follows:

SECURITY	(1)
10M - 210	(2)
5M - 205	(3)
200	(4)
190 - 210	(5)
6M - 210	(6)
2M - 200	(7)
3M6 - 210	(8)
(58,800)	(9)

This is how the blackboards are written. The explanation of each entry is given below.

(1)   security identification code which is not larger than seven letters.

(2)   volume -the best offer placed through the post (lowest selling price).

(3)   volume -the best bid placed through the post (highest buying price).

(4)   closing price.

(5)   limits in which the price can fluctuate without causing a suspension. Read Section II.G. for an understanding of this entry.

(6)   volume -the highest price of a transaction during the day.

(7)   volume -the lowest price of a transaction during the day.
(8)   volume -the price of the last transaction registered in the
        post.
(9)   share volume of the day.

For those stocks in which short-selling is permitted, there is an additional row of information.

Finally, there is another room in which the money market transactions are executed

G. SYSTEM OF PRICES SET BY THE EXCHANGE

First of all, it is necessary to define the concept of a base price to understand the system of prices set by the exchange.

The base price for a share is the one corresponding to the last transaction.

In order to avoid excessive and erractic price changes, the exchange has a system of base prices with allowed fluctuation between two parameters. The allowed limits of fluctuation are equal to the base price, plus and minus 5% of the base price, plus or minus the necessary adjustment to the nearest tick. When a transaction goes beyond the current limits, it will be suspended for 60 minutes and this fact will be announce by microphone.

During the suspension the transaction can be closed by a third party who improves the price within the limits of fluctuation. If this is the case, the suspended transaction will not be valid and the original limits will not change. If the transaction that originated the suspension is not closed by a third party and no other transaction is concerted in the period of suspension within the limits of fluctuation a new set of parameters will be fixed.

The new range of fluctuation will be determined considering as base price the upper or lower limit of the old range. The new limits will be equal to this new base price, plus and minus 5% of it, plus or minus the adjustment to the closest tick. If a transaction goes beyond these new limits, it will be suspended for 90 minutes following the procedure described.

Finally, the exchange does not permit a transaction that goes beyond two times the 5% limits of fluctuation.

H. COMMISSIONS

Brokers are entitled to commissions on all exchange-executed transacctions. The Mexican stock exchange has specified a fixed commission schedule, periodically revised, for all members. This means, a fixed rate for all customers of a given size regardless of which member firm handled the order.

Since June 1985, the commission for an average investor who buys or sells stock (spot or forward) is 1.7% if the transaction is below $ 200,000,000. If it is greater that this amount the fee is only 1%. However, the commission schedule applicable to commercial banks, insurance and bonding companies, credit auxiliar organizations, pension funds, and member of the exchange buying or selling for their own account is 0.85% regardless of the amount of the transaction. The commission use for mutual funds is only 0.50%. In any case, the minimun service will be $50.

The total commission is distributed as follows:

> 88.50 % for the brokerage house
> 6.25 % for the contingency fund
> 3.50 % for the Mexican stock exchange
> 1.50 % for the Mexican Association of Brokerage Houses
> 0.25 % for the Institute for the Stock Deposit
> ----------
> 100.00

Rule 10-78 of the National Securities Commission also authorizes the brokerage houses to charge a monthly fee for the custody and management of portfolios since June 1985. Currently, this fee is equal to $1,000 plus 0.0925 per million applicable to the value of the portfolio at the end of each month.

Two different schedules were in operations in the 1969-1985 period. This is important to remember because the database used in this work goes from 1972 to 1981. Tables II.7 and II.8 present these schedules showing lower rates than the current ones.

As the reader may have noticed, the exchange has maintanied a system of fixed commissions for stocks up until now. That is, if an investor wants to buy any listed stock, he or she will be charged the same commission whether he or she goes to any of the 25 brokerage houses or to the only broker. The absence of competition in terms of prices has led members of the exchange to compete with one another by offering a diversity of services to customers such as security analysis, quotation boards, research reports and account executives available for advice and information. Small member firms can not provide the same kind of services than the big ones. Thus, they are in an unfavorable position. This, in part can help explain why 10 brokerage houses concentrated 75.5% of all stock transacted in the exchange in 1990 (See Table II.9).

I propose a change from fixed to flexible commissions in the Mexican stock exchange. In this way, brokers will be free to set commissions at any desired rate or to negotiate with customers concerning the fees charge for particular trades. Firms will tend to specialize. Some of them will go "discount" dropping most services and cutting commissions. Others will offer a "full service" and charge a higher commission. The U. S. stock market terminated a system of fixed commissions by the Securities Acts Amendments of May 1, 1975. The experience after the "May day" has shown lower transaction costs and a wider range of alternatives for investors.

I. SIZE OF THE MARKET

Table II.10 presents the number of issues and companies listed in the Mexican stock exchange in different years. In the 1972-1981 period, the number of listed stocks went from 436 to 362 and the number of listed corporations from 371 to 240. Not only listed issues and companies have been decreasing, but the turnover has been high. However, this tendency was temporarly reversed with the 1987 boom in which the average market price/book value ratio went from 0.8 to 2.4 and the interest of corporations to become public increased slightly.

Until 1986 the tax policy permitted corporations to deduct interest payments. This fostered a bias against equity financing. In adittion, up until now the capital gains obtanied by individuals in the secondary market are tax exempt. In 1987 the government adopted a fiscal reform which only allows firms to deduct the real component of interest payments. There was a transitional period of four years in which the tax base was an average of the two systems.

The peso value of new issues of the first eight months of 1987 far surpasses the peso value of new issues of the last five years[7]. In spite of this, only a small part of the biggest 500 corporations are listed in the exchange.

Table II.11 shows other statistics that are useful to determine the size of the market such as : share volume, peso volume, their relationship with gross national product and the total peso volume of money and capital markets. Share volume increased steadly from 18 to 1,292 millions from 1972 to 1981. In the same period, the peso volume went up from 1,661 to 102,497 millions; the peso volume as a percentage of nominal gross national product increased from 0.29 to 1.74%, reaching a highest of 3.06% in the boom market of 1979; and finally, the peso volume of stock as a percentage of total volume of money and capital markets improved from 2.99 to 8.62%.

1982 was not a very good year for the market due primarily to the expropiation of the banking system. Banks were owners of part of many corporations' equities; then, when the government expropiated banks, all these equities were transfered to them. It took the government almost a year to complete the process in which most companies were returned to the private sector. Since then, the size of the stock market has expanded as the peso volume represented 8.17% of nominal gross national in 1990. However, the peso volume of stock as percentage of total volume of money and capital markets, in the 70's has pratically the same average as in the 80's.

---

[7] The figure is not adjusted for inflation.

J. SOME DESCRIPTIVE STATISTICS ON THE MARKET

The value of shares listed on the Mexican stock exchange was 180 billion pesos in July 25, 1991. It is almost impossible to get a series of the capitalization of the market that goes back to 1970. It is even harder to get one concerning the market value of corporate equities in Mexico. However, as it was mentioned in the last section, there are many of the 500 biggest Mexican corporations in terms of sales that are not yet listed in the exchange.

There is great concentration of value within the lists of stocks on the Mexican stock exchange. For example, the market value of TELMEX was 40.17 billion pesos in July 25, 1991. The second most valuable stock issue on the Mexican exchange was CEMEX whose value was 11.65 billions. The third one was CIFRA with a market value of 10.62 billions. The sum of these three corporations constitute near 35 % of the total value of the market.

Continuing with the supply of shares, it is important to mention that the group or family structure prevailing in the Mexican industry has discouraged corporations from being listed in the exchange. When they finally decide to go public, the group controls most of the shares and only a few percentage is freely traded. Heyman (1987) estimates that 80 % of all listed stock are held by the various groups and only 20 % of the shares are traded on a continuous basis.

On the demand side, there is not an exact figure of the number of participants in the 1970's. Executives of the exchange estimate that the number of investors was not greater than 10,000 in 1970 and near 25,000 in 1975. Since 1980 the Mexican Association of Brokerage Houses publishes data concerning its member firms and the number of acounts they deal with. In 1982, there were 66,000 separate market accounts registered with brokerage houses[8]. In November 1986, the number of accounts increased to 180,028 and a year later to 403,083. Since then, the number of accounts has been decreasing significantly to reach a level near to 120,000. The author estimates that the relative importance of trading by financial institutions and intermediaries has been rising rapidly and their weight in determining prices is much more important than the trading by individuals.

Table II.12 shows how the structure and number of intermediaries has changed over time. In 1973 there were three brokerage houses and 72 brokers. With the securities market law of 1975, new members of the exchange can only be organized as corporations. All the brokers who merged to form brokerage

---

[8] The majority of these accounts did not have stocks in their position.

houses were given advantages. That is why in 1979 there were only eight brokers and 31 brokerage houses. Today, the market has one broker and 25 brokerage houses. Table II.13 compares the equity, the total custody, the number of offices, the number of accounts, and the number of employees of the 25 brokerage houses. There are big differences among them and only a few dominate on each item. For example: 56 % of the sum of equities is concentrated on six brokerage houses; 60 % of the total custody is distributed among five houses; 55 % of the total number of offices belongs to 3 houses; and 55 % of the accounts corresponds to five houses.

It is necessary to include a discussion of the evolution of the stock index published by the exchange which can be used as a summary measure of the behavior of the market. Table II.14 presents the value of the index at the end of December from 1970 to 1990. During the 70's, the stock market as measured by the index was practically stagnant until the last part of 1977. On one hand, very few people knew the market as an investment alternative. As it was mentioned in section II.B, most people had a clear preference for fixed-income instruments (bonos) issued by banks. On the other hand, corporations did not have interest in going public and get financing through the stock market for fiscal reasons and for the fact that market prices were low. The results of this period can be seen by looking at the column of share volume on Table II.11 in which no significant change appeared until 1978.

There was a boom in the stock market from 1977 until the first quarter of 1979. The boom was based on the economic growth coming from high public investment supported by external debt. This was accompanied by an intensive campaign of the exchange in the media. The crash came in the second semester of 1979 and continued until 1982. The explanations for the crash were based in terms of overvalued stocks, significant increases in interest rates coming from higher inflation, the introduction of new money market instruments such as Treasury Bills and Petrobonds, the decline in oil prices, the devaluation of the peso, the establishment of exchange controls and the consequent capital flights. All this led to a recession and to high uncertanty about the future.

1983 was the beginning of a new bullish environment based mainly on the economic recovery, the fall in the inflation rate and the restructuring of the external debt. This tendency continued until the first part of 1986, date in which the most important Mexican stock boom started and lasted until October 6, 1987. Unlike the 1977-1979 boom, the 1986-1987 boom was accompanied by no economic growth, the return of capital from abroad, a three-digit inflation and a huge foreign debt. Besides, the number of investors involved and the volume transacted was much more important. The Mexican great crash came in a very short period of time and investors saw the index going down with a very small volume. The index dropped from 373,216 points in October 6, 1987 to 86,606 points in January 7, 1988, a decreased of 77 % in three months.

Finally, Table II.14 compares the percentage change in the stock index with the percentage change of the consumer price index. In the 1971-1990 period, the inflation rate has exceeded the percentage change in the stock index eight times. More will be said about real returns in section III.C.

CHART II.1
STRUCTURE OF THE MEXICAN FINANCIAL SYSTEM

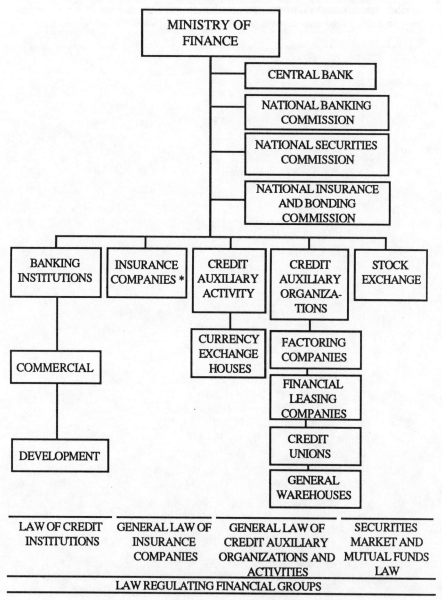

* The bonding companies are not considered here. However, they are part of the system because they are licensed by the Ministery of Finance.

CHART II.2
THE STOCK EXCHANGE

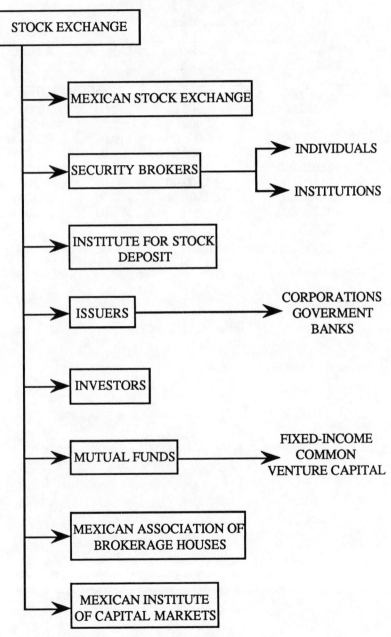

TABLE II.3
CURRENT ROUND LOTS AND TICKS
In operation since 07/1990

	MINIMUM PRICE			MAXIMUM PRICE	TICK	ROUND LOT
From $	1.00	to $		100.00 $	1.00	100,000 shares
	102.00			500.00	2.00	20,000 shares
	505.00			1,000.00	5.00	10,000 shares
	1,010.00			5,000.00	10.00	5,000 shares
	5,025.00			10,000.00	25.00	2,000 shares
	10,050.00			20,000.00	50.00	1,000 shares
	20,100.00			50,000.00	100.00	500 shares
	50,200.00			100,000.00	200.00	500 shares
	100,500.00			----	500.00	500 shares

TABLE II.4.A
ROUND LOTS AND TICKS
In operation from 08/1987 to 06/1990

	MINIMUM PRICE			MAXIMUM PRICE	TICK	ROUND LOT
From $	1.00	to $		100.00 $	1.00	50,000 shares
	105.00			500.00	5.00	10,000 shares
	510.00			1,000.00	10.00	5,000 shares
	1,025.00			5,000.00	25.00	1,000 shares
	5,050.00			10,000.00	50.00	500 shares
	10,100.00			20,000.00	100.00	500 shares
	20,500.00			50,000.00	500.00	250 shares
	51,000.00			100,000.00	1,000.00	100 shares
	100,000.00			----	5,000.00	50 shares

TABLE II.4.B
ROUND LOTS AND TICKS
In operation from 01/1987 to 07/1987

	MINIMUM PRICE			MAXIMUM PRICE	TICK	ROUND LOT
From $	0.05	to $		4.95 $	0.05	100 shares
	5.00			9.90	0.10	100 shares
	10.00			24.75	0.25	100 shares
	25.00			49.50	0.50	100 shares
	50.00			99.00	1.00	100 shares
	100.00			198.00	2.00	100 shares
	200.00			495.00	5.00	100 shares
	500.00			780.00	10.00	100 shares
	790.00			985.00	15.00	100 shares
	1,000.00			2,475.00	25.00	100 shares
	2,500.00			4,950.00	50.00	100 shares
	5,000.00			9,900.00	100.00	100 shares
	10,000.00			19,800.00	200.00	50 shares
	20,000.00			29,600.00	400.00	50 shares
	30,000.00			59,400.00	600.00	50 shares
	60,000.00			---	---	25 shares

TABLE II.5
ROUND LOTS
In Operation from 01/1982 to 12/1986

	MINIMUM PRICE		MAXIMUM PRICE	ROUND LOT
From $	0.05	to $	498.00	100 shares
	500.00		995.00	50 shares
	1,000.00		9,950.00	25 shares
	10,000.00		----	10 shares

TABLE II.6
PRICE INTERVALS
In Operation from 01/1982 to 12/1986

	MINIMUM PRICE		MAXIMUM PRICE	TICK
From $	0.05	to $	4.95 $	0.05
	5.00		9.90	0.10
	10.00		49.75	0.25
	50.00		99.50	0.50
	100.00		199.00	1.00
	200.00		498.00	2.00
	500.00		995.00	5.00
	1,000.00		4,990.00	10.00
	5,000.00		----	50.00

TABLE II.7
COMMISSIONS PER SHARE
In operation from 1969 to 1973

PRICE	FEE	PRICE	FEE
$ 10	0.30 $	190	1.55
20	0.40	200	1.60
30	0.50	210	1.65
40	0.60	220	1.70
50	0.70	230	1.75
60	0.80	240	1.80
70	0.90	250	1.85
80	1.00	260	1.90
90	1.05	270	1.95
100	1.10	280	2.00
110	1.15	290	2.05
120	1.20	300	2.10
130	1.25	310	2.15
140	1.30	320	2.20
150	1.35	330	2.25
160	1.40	340	2.30
170	1.45	350	2.35
180	1.50		

TABLE II.8
COMMISSIONS PER 100 SHARES *
In operation from 1973 to 1985

	MINIMUM PRICE		MAXIMUM PRICE	COMMISSIONS	
From $	0.00 to $	499.99 $	5.00	plus 4.00 %	
From $	500.00 to $	7,999.99 $	20.00	plus 1.00%	
From $	8,000.00 to $	99,999.99 $	60.00	plus 0.50%	
From $	100,000.00 to $	------ $	460.00	plus 0.10%	

The minimum commission was $ 25.00 per transaction.
This schedule was applicable to spot and forward transactions.
* The fee was proportional in the case of odd lots.

TABLE II.9
STOCK TRANSACTIONS PER MEMBER FIRM
Jan-Dec 1990

MEMBER	No. Of Transactions	Millions of Shares	Volume (Billions of pesos)	%
Acciones y Valores	27,725	3,115	9.3	13.4
Inverméxico	18,414	1,008	6.9	9.9
Inverlat	31,419	1,719	6.3	9.1
Grupo Bursatil Mexicano	18,503	1,359	5.8	8.3
Operadora de Bolsa	41,915	2,055	5.6	8.1
Inversora Bursatil	8,997	1,296	5.2	7.6
Probursa	37,456	1,993	3.7	5.4
Abaco	28,007	1,144	3.7	5.3
Interacciones	12,869	661	3.0	4.4
Cremi	12,525	405	2.8	4.0
15 Brokerage Houses and one agent	164,459	6,591	16.8	24.5
TOTAL	402,289	21,346	69.1	100.0

Source: 1990 Annual bulletin published by the Mexican stock exchange.

TABLE II.10
LISTED ISSUES AND CORPORATIONS ON THE MEXICAN STOCK
EXCHANGE *

	1972		1975		1978	
	ISSUES	No. of Co's	ISSUES	No. of Co's	ISSUES	No. of Co's
STOCKS	436	371	545	369	528	349
FIXED-INCOME	481	110	404	81	439	112
TOTAL	917	481	949	450	967	461

	1980		1981		1982	
	ISSUES	No. of Co's	ISSUES	No. of Co's	ISSUES	No. of Co's
STOCKS	537	264	362	240	305	215
FIXED-INCOME	124	48	170	66	118	55
TOTAL	661	312	532	306	423	270

	1985		1990	
	ISSUES	No. of Co's	ISSUES	No. of Co's
STOCKS	263	187	795	390
FIXED-INCOME	457	123	6,726	766
TOTAL	720	310	7,521	1,156

* taken from different annual bulletins published by the exchange

TABLE II.11
SIZE OF THE MARKET

	(1) Nominal G.N.P. (billions of pesos)	(2) Share Volume (millions of shares)	(3) Peso Volume (millions of pesos)	(4) Total Volume of Money and Capital Markets (billions of pesos)	(5) % (3)/(1)	(6) % (3)/(4)
1970	0.44	9	722	0.03	0.16	2.14
1971	0.49	11	831	0.04	0.17	2.14
1972	0.56	18	1,661	0.06	0.29	2.99
1973	0.69	24	2,494	0.08	0.36	3.31
1974	0.90	25	2,539	0.10	0.28	2.63
1975	1.10	40	3,685	0.11	0.33	3.24
1976	1.37	61	6,055	0.14	0.44	4.43
1977	1.85	72	5,784	0.17	0.31	3.42
1978	2.34	356	30,310	0.17	1.30	1.80
1979	3.07	807	93,795	0.36	3.06	26.32
1980	4.47	913	74,875	0.48	1.68	15.53
1981	6.13	1,292	102,497	1.19	1.67	8.62
1982	9.80	841	44,079	2.32	0.45	1.90
1983	17.88	1,200	134,590	6.16	0.75	2.19
1984	29.47	2,510	370,879	15.36	1.26	2.41
1985	47.39	15,132*	1,130,935*	25.44	2.39	4.45
1986	79.54	33,211*	3,700,878*	75.68	4.65	4.89
1987	193.70	19,089*	23,024,828*	307.77	11.89	7.48
1988	392.71	43,424*	17,545,288*	965.82	4.47	1.82
1989	516.71(p)	90,369*	35,778,812*	1,170.28	6.92	3.06
1990	668.69(p)	154,241*	54,600,678*	2,279.15	8.17	2.40

*   it also includes common mutual funds
(p)   provisional
(1)   taken from the 1986 and 1990 annual reports of the central bank
(2), (3) and (4) were taken from different annual bulletins published by the Mexican stock exhange.

TABLE II.12
MEMBERS OF THE MEXICAN STOCK EXCHANGE

	1973	1976	1977	1978	1979	1980	1981
BROKERS	72	27	20	14	8	7	6
BROKERAGE HOUSES	3	10	24	27	31	31	31
TOTAL	75	37	44	41	39	38	37

	1982	1983	1984	1985	1986	1987	1990
BROKERS	6	6	6	6	6	6	1
BROKERAGE HOUSES	31	31	29	28	26	26	25
TOTAL	37	37	35	34	32	32	26

Source: annual bulletins published by the Mexican stock exchange

TABLE II.13
SOME DESCRIPTIVE STATISTICS
ON BROKERAGE HOUSES
May 1991

BROKERAGE HOUSE	EQUITY (millions)	CUSTODY (billions)	BRANCH OFFICES	No.OF ACCOUNTS	No. OF EMPLOYEES
Inverlat	556,661	19.11	28	24,315	1,015
Accival	550,505	20.95	6	12,435	346
O.B.S.A.	475,634	17.36	54	29,177	1,421
G.B.M.	407,408	4.86	3	3,437	249
Inbursa	305,707	15.03	1	2,889	143
Probursa	300,380	16.61	25	18,187	1,113
Inverméxico	246,805	8.57	4	3,944	328
C.B.I.	226,080	1.62	5	4,172	275
Interacciones	198,577	5.53	3	3,595	221
Finamex	154,799	1.86	5	6,189	249
Abaco	153,311	4.78	4	10,922	336
Multivalores	140,050	4.44	3	4,350	403
Arka	114,874	2.39	4	4,514	281
Accibur	91,769	3.68	3	7,738	271
Prime	83,233	2.31	4	3,821	262
Vector	80,865	3.98	3	4,527	262
Valburmex	75,171	1.90	9	3,140	237
Bursamex	72,964	2.00	3	3,576	234
Estrategia	62,646	1.74	5	2,918	289
Value	60,304	1.12	6	3,701	214
Fimsa	59,681	0.63	2	1,284	111
Afin	57,265	1.80	2	1,988	227
Cremi	52,717	2.38	7	3,535	229
México	51,141	1.63	1	2,090	153
Mexival	50,964	0.94	2	5,121	206
TOTAL	4,629,511	147.22	196	171,565	9,083

Source: Brokerage Houses Highlighs published by the Mexican Association of Brokerage Houses.

TABLE II.14
EVOLUTION OF THE STOCK INDEX

YEAR	VALUE OF THE STOCK INDEX (end of Dec.)(1)	PERCENTAGE CHANGE	% CHANGE OF C.P.I. (Dec. to Dec.)(2)
1970	147.47		
1971	139.74	- 5.24	5.2
1972	177.70	27.16	5.5
1973	184.74	3.96	21.3
1974	207.99	12.59	20.7
1975	213.65	2.72	11.2
1976	274.81	28.63	27.2
1977	388.37	41.32	20.7
1978	889.06	128.92	16.2
1979	1,347.14	51.52	20.0
1980	1,432.24	6.32	29.8
1981	947.87	- 33.81	28.7
1982	676.35	- 28.65	98.9
1983	2,451.93	262.52	80.8
1984	4,038.43	64.70	59.2
1985	11,197.17	177.27	63.7
1986	47,101.03	320.65	105.7
1987	105,669.95	124.35	159.2
1988	211,531.78	100.18	51.7
1989	418,925.13	98.04	19.7
1990	628,790.34	50.10	29.9

****

(1) Source: annual bulletins published by the exchange
(2) Source: Bank of Mexico, Serie "Estadisticas Historicas"

CHAPTER III

THE BEHAVIOR OF STOCK MARKET RETURNS

The Mexican stock market is growing. It is becoming an important mechanism in the creation and transfer of financial assets and liabilities. However, it is still developing and has several problems which must be solved if it is to fullfil its objectives. One problem is that of disinformation. Although the exchange publishes daily, weekly, monthly and annual bulletins, the information is not made available rapidly and inexpensively to all investors[9]. Furthermore, historical information is not nicely organized and contained in a magnetic tape or any other medium of rapid access for academicians, researchers or the general public[10].

The aforesaid makes it clear that there is a need for better and more affordable methods of information regarding the inner working of the Mexican exchange. In addition, the exchange, perhaps in cooperation with governments and universities should invest more in information that can be used by researchers to test the validity of different theories in an effort to explain the behavior of the market. Such information should be contanied in any means that is compatible with statistical and econometric packages that help process the necessary estimates to test hypotheses.

A. DATA

To my knowledge, the first attempt to process information regarding adjusted prices of stocks listed on the exchange was made by the

---

[9]Until 1986, only part of the information contanied in these bulletins was published in some national newspapers. Furthermore, there are only two financial newspapers, which are not available in some parts of the country.

[10] This statement is based on an interview with Ismael Alvarez who leads the Information and Publications Department at the Mexican exchange. He also mentioned that there is file contaning information regarding issues and transactions of the previous five years. This data is used by stockbrokerage houses which have terminals connected to the exchange.

Instituto Tecnológico Autónomo de México (I.T.A.M.) in 1983. A file was created containing weekly and monthly information of 91 stocks for time periods from 1972 to 1981. The file contains the following entries:

a) Week or month.

b) Closing price of the stock. Wednesday is used for weekly data and the first day of operations for monthly data. In any case where the closing Wednesday's price is not available, the closing price on Thursday is used.

c) Cash dividend paid net of taxes. If the efective payment day is not Wednesday for the weekly data, the cash dividend is registered as part of next week dividend. A similar criterion applies to monthly data.

Before the dividend is paid, it is declared. When a firm declares a cash dividend, it is supposed to withold and pay taxes for the shareholder.

d) Stock dividend. In this particular case the firm pays, for instance, one share for each ten. The entry will have this information expressed as a ratio, 1/10=0.10. If the effective payment day is not Wednesday for the weekly data, the stock dividend is registred as part of the next week's dividend. A similar criterion applies to monthly data.

e) Subscription. Here, the firms gives the opportunity to its shareholders to buy a fixed number of shares (in proportion to the existing shares) at a specific price. There are two pieces of information that correspond to this item. One is the proportion and the other is the subscription price. For example if the company authorizes a subscription of one share for each five outstanding at a price of $100.00; then, 0.20 will be the proportion and $100.00 will the subscription price. If the effective payment day is not Wednesday for the weekly data, the subscription is registered as part ofthe following week's information. A similar criterion applies to monthly data.

f) Stock split. When there is a split, the firm subdivides its shares, exchanging the old ones for a number (generally greater) of new ones. If there is a stock split of two-to-one, a two will appear in the corresponding column. If there is no split in a certain week, the column will have a one to indicate this event.

g) Adjusted price. It is neccesary to adjust the closing market prices in order to determine returns correctly. To describe the neccesary adjustments, the following symbols should first be introduced:

$$Pt = \text{closing market price}$$
$$d\$ = \text{cash dividend}$$
$$ds = \text{stock dividend}$$
$$Ps = \text{subscription price}$$
$$Pro = \text{subscription proportion}$$
$$Sp = \text{split}$$

$$Pa = \text{adjusted price}$$

Now the adjustments:

For cash dividends Pa =   Pt + d$
For stock dividends Pa =   Pt (1 + ds)
For subscriptions   Pa =   Pt (1 + Pro) - Pro (Ps)
For splits   Pa =   Pt (Spl)
For simulatenous adjustments
                Pa =   (Spl + ds + Pro) + d$ - Pro (Ps)

h) Rate of return. The rate of return for week t on a given stock is

$$Rit = \frac{Pat+1 - Pt}{Pt}$$

A sample of the data and the way the adjusted prices and rates of return are calculated is given below.

ALFA 1979
Subscription

W	Pt	d$	ds	Prop	Ps	Spl	Pa	Rit
1	668	0.00	0.00	0.00	0	1	668.0000	0.05453
2	694	10.43	0.00	0.00	0	1	704.4300	0.03170
3	716	0.00	0.00	0.00	0	1	716.0000	0.05553
4	748	0.00	0.00	0.70	630	1	755.7644	0.02941
5	770	0.00	0.00	0.00	0	1	770.0000	0.12987
6	870	0.00	0.00	0.00	0	1	870.0000	-0.03678
7	838	0.00	0.00	0.00	0	1	838.0000	-0.01306
8	158	0.00	0.23	0.00	0	5	827.0510	0.06329
9	168	0.00	0.00	0.00	0	1	168.0000	-0.06547
10	157	0.00	0.00	0.00	0	1	157.0000	0.01910

Tables III.1 and III.2 present the stock data details for weekly and monthly returns respectively.

Unfortunately the initial attempt was not followed within the I.T.A.M.. As a result the file is not up to date now and it includes some stocks that are delisted or that became inactive.

This work expands the entries of the file to include :
a) a market value index
b) an equally weighted index
c) the return on different portfolios

d) the return on a risk-free asset
e) information concerning trading frequencies
f) information regarding transaction costs
g) the inflation rate
h) the exchange rate between the Mexican peso and the American dollar
i) returns from some American securities and indexes

B. INDEXES AND PORTFOLIOS

The old stock price index published by the exchange was based on fixed sample of 29 stocks. The names of the stocks included in this index are presented in Table III.3. The data file used in this dissertation include all but two of them (AHMSA and TELMEX). The exchange used a constant factor for each stock in the sample to calculate the index. The value of each constant factor was determined at the time the index was implemented as follows:

$$Fo^i = \frac{100}{\text{price of the stock at the time the index was implemented}}$$

Thus, the constant factor of stock i is equal to the number of shares that one can buy with \$100. The constant factor was adjusted for cash dividends, stock dividends and splits. It was not adjusted for subscriptions. The factor weighted stocks taking only their price into consideration. Then, the most heavily weighted stocks were AVIA, APAS, and KIMB.

The sum of the multiplication between the closing price of each of the 29 stocks and its corresponding constant factor is divided by the same operation using yesterday's prices and constant factors. The resulting factor is then multiplied by yesterday's index value to obtain today's index. Expressed as:

$$I(t) = I(t-1) \frac{\sum F_t^i P_t^i}{\sum F_{t-1}^i P_{t-1}^i}$$

where:

$I(t)$ = the value of the old index at time t

I(t-1)   = the value of the old index at time t-1

F_t^i = the constant factor of stock i at time t

P_t^i = the closing price of stock i at time t

F_{t-1}^i = the constant factor of stock i at time t-1

P_{t-1}^i = the closing price of stock i at time t-1

The index was in operation until September 19, 1980. It was modified because a structural change took place at the end of the 70's in the sense that the listed stocks were different. Therefore, the fixed sample was not representative of issues and volume anymore. Besides, it was necessary to improve the relative weight of each stock because the old index considered price, but not the number of shares outstanding.

The new index uses a dynamic sample of stocks that is revised every other month. The sample for July-August of 1991 consist of 40 stocks[11]. The list of the stocks forming the sample is presented in Table III.4. The stocks in the sample are those having higher liquidity, higher percentage held by the public, and price variability similar to the variability of the market. This new index weights stocks using both price and number of shares outstanding using the following method of valuation:

$$I(t) = I(t-1) \frac{\sum P_t^i \, Q_{t-1}^i \, F_t^i}{\sum P_{t-1}^i \, Q_{t-1}^i}$$

---

[11] The number of stocks in the sample has changed over time. For instance, it was increasead from 42 to 47 in July of 1987 and from 47 to 52 in November of 1987.

where:

$I(t)$ = the value of the index at time t

P_t^i = the price of stock i at time t

Q_t^i = the number of outstanding shares of stock i at time t

F_t^i = adjusting factor

The index is adjusted for : a) cash dividends, b) stock dividends, c) subscriptions, d) splits, e) conversion of debentures into common stocks, f) conversion of preferred stock into common stock, and g) repurchase agreements. The index is adjusted either in the numerator or in the denominator depending upon the specific event generating the adjustment[12].

Portfolios were formed using the data from both the weekly and monthly returns. Only those stocks that had observations over the 1972-1981 time period were considered in both cases. That is, 34 stocks were considered in forming portfolios on weekly returns, and 37 stocks were used to form portfolios with the monthly returns.

Using weekly returns, four portfolios of seven stocks each, one portfolio of six stocks, and an equally weighted portfolio of the 34 stocks, were formed. Using the monthly returns, three portfolios of seven stock each, two eight-stock portfolios, and an equally weighted portfolio of the 37 stocks, were formed.

C. DISTRIBUTION OF STOCK MARKET RETURNS

The return next period on a share of common stock is not known and it can be thought of as a random variable. In other words, the return can be properly considered as a variable whose observed value is governed by a probability distribution. Statistically speaking, returns are random

---

[12] See the booklet published by the exchange for a more detailed explanation of how the adjustments are performed.

variables that can be examined by the process which generates its probability distribution, which in turn, can be described in terms of its paramenters that must be estimated from a sample.

In finance, as in many other disciplines, not only are the true parameters (mean, variance, etc.) unknown, but the type of distribution that generates a sample is also unknown. Very often it is assumed that returns follow a normal distribution. This is done partly because statistical techniques for analyzing data from normal distributions are abundant relative to the techniques that are available to analyze data from non-normal distributions. Besides, much of the derivation of the theory (i.e., C.A.P.M.) is simpler when normality is assumed.

The problem in question is an empirical one that has been studied to a great extent in the U.S.A.. Roberts (1959) found that a series of randomly generated price changes would very closely resemble actual stock data. Osborne (1959) recommended that one should study price changes in logarithmic form. His model showed that logarithmic price changes conform to the random walk model. That is, he showed that logarithmic price changes could be considered as an independent and identically distributed random variable with finite variances. At this time, most researchers combined the above results with the theorem of the central limit to assume that distributions of price changes follow a normal distribution. Mandelbrot (1963), in a rather complex paper disputed the assumption of normality arguing that, if one does not assume finite variances, the central limit theorem leads to a stable class of distributions of which the normal is a special case. Stable distributions are unaffected by addition. Thus, distributions of monthly and daily price changes would have the same general characteristics. This work was follow by Fama and Roll (1968,1971), Fisher and Lorie (1970), etc..

Fama (1965) showed frequency distributions for continously compounded daily returns for each of the 30 stocks of the Dow-Jones Industrial Average for time periods from 1957 to 1962. He rejected the hypothesis of normality for the daily returns. The frequency distribution of the sample is more peaked than the normal and assigns higher probabilities to extreme observations. He also indicated that the distributions of daily returns are very close to symmetric.

Fama (1976) found that the frequency distributions of simple monthly returns are slightly skewed to the right. Abstracting from the effects of differential sample sizes, he compared the relative frequencies of monthly and daily returns. He showed that distributions of monthly returns are less peaked about their mean and that the relative frequencies of extreme observations are smaller than for the daily returns. He concludes:

"Thus, contrary to the implications of the hypothesis that daily and monthly returns conform roughly to the same type of stable nonnormal distribution, monthly returns have distributions closer to normal than daily returns"[13].

Clark (1973), Morgan (1976), Westerfield, Tauchen and Pitts (1983), and Harris (1986, 1987) have examined price changes or returns with volume in the "Mixture of Distribution Hypothesis". Their results show that the hypothesis can explain why the sample distribution of daily price changes is kurtotic relative to normal. It is also able to provide the reason for a positively skewed distribution of the associate volume of trade.

Going from individual stocks to portfolios, the results of Blume (1968) and Officer (1971) showed that distributions of portfolio returns are of the same type as distributions of returns on securities.

Unfortunately, these studies have not been performed in the Mexican stock market. Therefore, we do not known if the normal distribution is a good approximation for weekly or monthly securities and portfolio returns. The purpose of this section is to calculate statistics that will determine the characteristics of the distributions of weekly and monthly returns.

A partial summary of some statistics regarding the distribution of weekly returns for 34 Mexican stocks contained in Tables III.5, III.6, and III.7 is presented below:

	1972-1981 91 stocks	1972-1976 34 stocks	1977-1981 34 stocks
average mean	0.0058	0.0037	0.0077
average standard deviation	0.0686	0.0532	0.0786

The average mean and standard deviation of weekly returns in the 1977-1981 period are higher than their respective values in the 1972-1976 period. This may be an indication of the presence of heteroscedasticity in the weekly return series. The average weekly mean return of .37% for the 1972-1976 period corresponds to an annual average return of 21.42%. The average annual change in the consumer price index (the inflation rate) over the same period was 17.08%. Real returns from investing in the

---

[13] Eugene F. Fama, "Foundations of Finance" Basic Books, 1976, pp. 33.

stock market were higher in the 1977-1981 period, considering that the annual average return of 49.09% (average weekly mean return of .77%) was higher than the 22.99% average annual change in inflation.

Means and standard deviations are calculated on simple returns (R) whereas skewness[14] and kurtosis[15] coefficients as well as the studentized range statistic[16] are calculated on continously compounded

---

[14] If a frequency distribution is not symmetrical, it is said to be skewed. A series is to be skewed in the direction of extreme values, or, speaking in terms of the curve, in the direction in which the excess tail appears. The skewness statistic will take on a value of zero when the distribution is completely symmetric. A positive value indicates that the observations are clustered more to the left of the mean with most of the extreme values to the right. When this is the case, the series is said to be skewd to the right. A negative value indicates that the series is skewed to the left. Relative skewness can be measured in many different ways: a) It can be measured based on percentiles. b) Skewness = (mean - mode) / standard deviation. c) Skewness = 3 (mean - median) / standard deviation. d) Skewness can be measured based on the third moment using the following formula:

$$\text{Skewness} = \frac{\sum_{i=1}^{N} \left((X_i - \overline{X}) / S_x \right)^3}{N}$$

[15] Kurtosis is a measure of the relative peakedness (leptokurtic) or flatnes (platykurtic) of the curve. The basis of reference is the normal distribution (mesokurtic) which has a kurtosis of zero. If the kurtosis is positive, the distribution is more peaked than a normal distribution. A negative value means that it is flatter. The common formula to calculate kurtosis based on the fourth moment is:

$$\text{Kurtosis} = \frac{\sum_{i=1}^{N} \left((X_i - \overline{X}) / S_x \right)^4}{N} - 3$$

[16] The studentized range statistic = (maximum - minimum) /st. dev.. This tests the assumption of normality. There is a table that shows

returns [Ln (1+R)]. The always positive difference between R and Ln (1 + R) is greater the further R is from zero in either direction. Using continuously compounded returns would tend to pull in the right tails and strech out the left tails of the distribution of simple returns. This would make the distribution more symmetrical.

Table III.5 shows that only four out of the 34 individual securities have a skewness statistic within a two-standard error bound. Of the remaining 30 significant coefficients, 17 are positive and 13 are negative. This indicates that most of the weekly returns on individual stocks are skewed one way or another. The table also shows that none of the stocks has a kurtosis statistic within a two-standard error bound. This means that all of the distributions of individual stock returns are more peaked than normal distributions in the 1972-1981 period. In addition, the studentized range tests was performed to detect fat tails. In all cases, the studentized range statistics exceeds the 95% fractile of the distribution. Thus, the hypothesis that the return series is normally distributed is rejected in favor of the hypothesis that the sample comes from a distribution that is "fat-tailed" relative to a normal.

Table III.8 presents the statistics regarding the distributions of weekly portfolios and indexes. The correlation coefficient between the index based on 29 stocks published by the exchange and an equally weighted portfolio of the 34 stocks with observations in the 1972-1981 period is 0.83. Note that the market index has a lower mean and a higher standard deviation than the equally weighted portfolio. The distribution of portfolios returns as well as the equally weighted portfolio are skewed to the right and leptokurtic as one can deduce from the corresponding statistics.

Statistics regarding the distribution of monthly returns for 37 Mexican stocksare presented in Tables III.9, III.10, and III.11. Table III.9 shows that in the 1972-1981 period 24 out of the 37 individual securities have a skewness coefficient within a two-standard error bound. This indicates that most individual monthly returns follow distributions that are symmetrical. The table also shows that only three out of 37 stocks have a kurtosis coefficient within a two-standard error bound. This is a clear indication that most of the distributions of monthly returns are more peaked than normal. The studentized range test was also used for detecting fat tails. In 33 out of the 37 stocks, the studentized range statistic exceeds the 95% fractile of the distribution, and the hypothesis that the return series is normally distributed is rejected in favor of the hypothesis that the

---

fractiles of the lower and upper tails of sampling distributions of the sutundetized range, when this is computed from samples from normal distributions.

sample comes from a distribution that is "fat-tailed" relative to a normal distribution. Tables III.10 and III.11 presents the same statistics for the two five-year subperiods.

Finally, Tables III.12, III.13, and III.14 show the statistics regarding monthly portfolios. They present evidence that the distribution of portfolio are symmetrical and slightly peaked over the 1972-1981 period. However, in the two five-year subperiods analyzed, the first four moments of the distribution of monthly portfolio seem to be very different.

D THE EFFECTS OF DIVERSIFICATION

One could distinguish between price changes which can be atributed to the market as a whole, called systematic risk, and those which are independent or that do not appear to be related to general market fluctuations, called unsystematic risk[17]. The former is a relative measure of the price volatility of a company's shares to the market as a whole. Its value is known as beta and it will be discussed in Chapter IV. The latter is associated with events unique to a particular corporation such as strikes, managerial expertise, and so forth.

The unsystematic risk can be reduced by diversification within the stock market. Up to a point, the spreading of funds over a number of stocks will reduce risk more than propotionately to the reduction in return. This is based on the fact that the correlation among stocks is not perfect. To demonstrate this principle among Mexican stocks, the 37x37 correlation matrix is presented in Table III.15. Only ten out the 666 coefficients have a negative sign and the average correlation coefficient is 0.24. Therefore, diversification causes the risk associated with each individual stock to be diminished in comparison with the overall portfolio risk. However, if an investor has a well-diversified portfolio, its systematic risk cannot be reduced by adding more stocks to the portfolio. That is, the systematic risk can only be controlled through diversification up to a certain point[18].

Since unsystematic risk can be diversified away, it is logical to raise the empirical question of how much diversification is necessary to effectively reduce it in the Mexican stock market. The monthly data on the 37 stocks with observations over the 1972-1981 period was used to answer the question. Securities were drawn randomly without replacement and portfolios holding from one to 37 stocks were constructed. Each portfolio was equally weighted and its mean and standard deviation were calculated. In order to reduce the dependence on single samples, the exercise was repeated ten times, and the average mean and standard deviation were used. Table III.16 shows the effects of

---

[17] For more detailed discussion the reader is refer to: W. F. Sharpe, "Capital Asset Prices: A Theory of Market Equilibrium Under Conditions of Risk," Journal of Finance, (September 1964): 425-42.

[18] The investor may reduce the systematic risk by liquidating some equity positions in order to purchase other securities such as: petrobonds, debentures, commercial paper, fixed-income mutual funds, or in order to buy real assets.

changing the number of stocks in a Mexican portfolio, describing an asympotically declining standard deviation as portfolio sizes increases. This asymptote approximates .067 which is the average systematic variation of the equally-weighted 37-stock portfolio shown in Table III.12.

Using 0.067 as a benchmark, which is very close to the standard deviation of the market index (0.064), the results show that almost all of the unsystematic risk is eliminated by the time the twentieth stock was added to the portfolio. This is much greater than the number that Evans and Archer (1968) found for the American stock market. They presented evidence showing that much of the unsystematic variation is eliminated by the time the eighth security is added to the portfolio. On the other hand, Fama (1976) found that almost all diversification was obtained after the 10-15 stocks were randomly selected. Another empirical paper demostrating the effects of diversification on risk was written by Wagner and Lau (1971) who demonstrated that as a result of diversification, portfolios consisting of large numbers of higher risk securities may be less risky than portfolios consisting of small numbers of low risk stocks, yet earn a substantially higher rate of return. Statman (1987) contradicted the widely accepted notion that the benefits of diversification in the United States are virtually exhausted when a portfolio contains approximately ten stocks. He showed that a well-diversified portfolio of randomly chosen stocks must include at least 30 stocks for a borrowing investors and 40 stocks for a lending investor.

The same experiment was repeated using weekly returns and the results showed that most of the unsysyematic risk was elimimated by the time the 16th. stock was added to the portfolio. Knowing that much of the unsystematic risk in the Mexican stock market is eliminated by holding a portfolio of approximately 16-20 stocks, the obvious question is : What is the average number of stocks contained in portfolios held by market participants? To answer this question, is important to differentiate among three types of investors. First, those individual investors who put all or most of their money in a stock mutual fund (common mutual fund) hold portfolios with at least ten stocks. This is because the law prohibits that these mutual funds invest more than 10% of their equity in one single stock. However, most common mutual funds have a higher number of stocks than the required by the National Securities Commission. Therefore, one can conclude that individual investors in common mutual funds hold well-diversified portfolios. Second, institutional investors are subject to rules very similar to those applicable to common mutual funds; then, as a first approximation they also hold well-diversified portfolios. Third, there is no reliable information concerning the size of the portfolio on those individual investors who form their own or do so with help from their account executives. This, as well as the relative importance of each group of investors, would be an area for further research.

Practical experience suggests that most of investors in the third group hold imperfectly diversified portfolios. It seems like they are concerned not with the number of stocks per se, but with the composition of their portfolio (the number of different stock held). Then, they perfom a cost- benefit analysis to determine the incremental increases in the number of stock included in their portfolio.

E. EXTENDED DIVERSIFICATION

The financial instruments I have discussed so far have been Mexican peso-denominated investments. The purchase of a dollar-denominated security by a Mexican requires the prior purchase of dollars. In this particular case, ther is uncertainty with respect to the future value of the American security and the rate of exchange. For this reason, the return on a foreign investment may be subdivided into two parts. The first part is represented by the change in value of the foreign security in its own currency. The second part is represented by the change in the value of the foreign currency relative to the domestic currency of the investor. If the standard deviation of each part could be given as an indication of its risk, one could say in Mexico in the last ten years, the second part has been more volatile than the first one, and thus much more important in determining foreign returns. This may no be true in the 1972-1981 period.

However, part of the variability of foreign exchange price may be diversifiable if some correlation between the foreign exchange rates are negative or less than perfect. In the 1972-1981 period, the foreign exchange risk of a particular outcome could have been eliminated in Mexico by covering transactions. However, this opportunity was voided in 1982 with the imposition of exchange rate controls.

A method to determine whether or not international diversification contributes to lowering the risk of a portfolio, is to calculate the correlation of returns on equities in one country with the returns on equities in another country. The benefits from diversification might be stronger the lower the correlations among common stocks or indexes of different countries. Another way is to determine the extent of the benefits of diversification in an individual domestic stock market and then to consider the additional reduction in variability that would occur from the construction of an international portfolio [Solnik (1974); Levy and Sarnat (1970)].

This section investigates the opportunities that may be available to a Mexican investing part of his or her portfolio in American securities. The data for American stocks was obtained from the C.R.S.P. monthly tape. From the 30 Dow-Jones stocks, 21 not missing an observation in the period 1972-1982 were selected as well as the Standard and Poor's market-value index. The 21 American stocks were combined with the 37 Mexican stocks to form a 58x58 correlation-coefficient matrix. For the sake of simplicity, the 1,653 correlation coefficients are not presented here. It is sufficient to say that the average correlation coefficents of the matrix is 0.17. The correlation coefficient between the American and the

Mexican Index is 0.10. Both of them are lower than the average correlation of Mexican securities calculated in the previous section (0.24) establishing the benefits that can be obtanied by international diversification.

Section III.D. determined the extent of the benefits of diversification in the Mexican stock market. Two possiblities arise in exploring the reduction of risk that can be obtained by diversifying a portfolio internationally. First, the risk of an investment in an American stock can be assumed to be due only to price variablity and not to exhange rate fluctuations. The exchange risk can be removed by hedging foreign holdings or by buying a forward exchange contract. Second, if a Mexican investing in American stocks does not protect himself against exchange rate fluctuations, he is in fact speculating in both stock price changes and currencies.

Table III.17 shows the effects of an extended hedged diversification for a Mexican investor. Both Mexican and American stocks were drawn randomly without replacement and international portfolios holding from one to 58 securities were constructed. Each portfolio was equally weighted and their mean and standard deviation were calculated. This excercise was repeated ten times and the average mean and standard deviation were used in order to reduce the dependence on single samples. Compare the (average mean) / (average st. dev.) ratio of a Mexican portfolio containing 20 stocks which is presented in table III.16 with the (aerage-mean) / (average st. dev.) of a 20-stock-international-portfolio which is given in Table II.17. This is the Sharpe's mu/sigma measure of risk adjusted return in which risk-averse investors prefer a higher ratio. The results of this comparison do not support the benefits of international diversification. In fact, they show a small loss in going from a domestic portfolio with an index of 0.32 to an international portfolio with an index of 0.31.

Table III.18 presents the effects of an extended unhedged diversification available to a Mexican investing part of his or her portfolio in American stocks. Therefore, risks and returns are going to be calculated in Mexican pesos. The same procedure was used to form portfolios with the following exception: when an American stock was selected, pesos were converted to dollars at the prevailing exchange rate at the begining of the month and they were reconverted into pesos at the end of the month. This process was accomplished by adjusting the returns on American stocks as follows :

$$R(US) + [S1 - So/ So] + R(US) \times [S1 - So/So]$$

where:

$R(US)$ is the rate of return on American stocks,

[S1 - So/So] is the rate of return on the dollar in terms of pesos.

As expected, the risk and the mean of an international portfolio unprotected against exchange risk is greater than for a covered international portfolio. However, it standard deviation is still much smaller than for a comparable Mexican portfolio. The reason for this is that the rate of return on the dollar in terms of pesos [S1 - So/So] was not significantly correlated to the rate of return on American stocks, as can be deduced from Table III.19.

TABLE III.1

STOCK DATA DETAILS FOR WEEKLY RETURNS

****

SECURITY I.D. CODE	NAME OF THE FIRM	TYPE OF OPERATION	SERIES	PERIOD FROM	PERIOD TO
ACCI	FONDO ACCIVALMEX, S.A.	FINANCE	ORD.	11/80	12/81
ACCO	ANDERSON CLAYTON	NONDURABLE GOODS	ORD.	1/72	12/81
ACEY	FUNDIDORA DE ACEROS TEPEYAC, S.A	METAL INDUSTRY	ORD.	1/72	12/81
ALFA	GRUPO INDUSTRIAL ALFA, S.A.	INDUSTRIAL GROUP	ORD.	8/78	12/78
			B	1/79	12/81
ALTR	ALTRO, S.A. DE C.V.	NONDURABLE GOODS	A	10/78	12/78
			A*	1/79	12/81
ALUM	ALUMINIO, S.A.	METAL INDUSTRY	A*	1/72	12/81
APAS	CEMENTOS APASCO, S.A.	CONSTRUCTION	A	1/72	12/81
AURR	AURRERA, S.A.	RETAIL TRADE	A	12/76	12/81

****

TABLE III.1 (CONTINUED)

****

SECURITY I.D. CODE	NAME OF THE FIRM	TYPE OF OPERATION	SERIES	PERIOD FROM	PERIOD TO
AUTL	COMPAÑIA MINERA AUTLAN	MINING	A*	5/75	12/76
			B*	1/77	12/79
			A*	1/80	12/81
AVIA	COMPAÑIA MEXICANA DE AVIACION, S.A.	SERVICES	ORD.	1/72	12/73
			*	1/74	12/81
BACA	BACARDI Y COMPANIA, S.A.	NONDURABLE GOODS	*	1/72	12/81
BANA	BANAMEX, S.A.	FINANCE	ORD.	1/72	12/81
BANC	BANCOMER, S.A.	FINANCE	ORD.	1/78	12/81
BCH	BANCO DE CEDULAS HIPOTECARIAS, S.A.	FINANCE	ORD.	1/72	12/81
BDCO	BANCO DE COMERCIO	FINANCE	ORD.	1/72	10/77
BIMB	GRUPO INDUSTRIAL BIMBO, S.A.	NONDURABLE GOODS	ORD.	2/80	12/81
BIME	BICICLETAS DE MEXICO, S.A.	NONDURABLE GOODS	ORD.	1/72	12/76
			ORD.	1/80	12/81

****

TABLE III.1 (CONTINUED)

****

SECURITY I.D. CODE	NAME OF THE FIRM	TYPE OF OPERATION	SERIES	PERIOD FROM	PERIOD TO
CAME	CAMESA, S.A.	METAL INDUSTRY	ORD.	9/78	12/78
			A	1/79	12/81
CAMP	CAMPOS HERMANOS S.A.	METAL INDUSTRY	ORD.	1/72	12/81
CANA	COMPAÑIA MINERA DE CANANEA	MINING	A*	12/72	12/81
CANN	CANNON MILLS. S.A.	NONDURABLE GOODS	ORD.	1/72	5/81
			*	6/81	12/81
CARB	UNION CARBIDE MEXICANA, S.A	CHEMICALS	A	1/72	12/76
			A*	1/77	12/81
CECH	CELULOSA DE CHIHUAHUA, S.A.	PAPER AND ALLIED PROD.	ORD.	1/72	12/79
CELA	CELANESE MEXICANA, S.A.	CHEMICALS	A*	1/72	12/81
CEME	CEMENTOS MEXICANOS, S.A.	CONSTRUCTION	A	7/78	12/81
CENM	CENTRAL DE MALTA, S.A.	NONDURABLE GOODS	ORD.	1/72	12/81

****

TABLE III.1 (CONTINUED)

****

SECURITY I.D. CODE	NAME OF THE FIRM	TYPE OF OPERATION	SERIES	PERIOD FROM	PERIOD TO
CERM	CERVECERIA MOCTEZUMA, S.A.	NONDURABLE GOODS	ORD.	1/72	12/81
CIGA	CIGARROS LA TABACALERA MEXICANOS	NONDURABLE GOODS	A*	10/76	12/81
CODU	CONDUMEX, S.A.	ELECTRICAL EQUIPMENT	A*	11/77	12/81
COME	MULTIBANCO COMERMEX,S.A.	FINANCE	ORD.	1/78	12/81
COMZ	COMERCIAL EUZKADI, S.A.	CHEMICALS	A*	1/78	12/81
CONF	BANCA CONFIA, S.A.	FINANCE	ORD.	5/79	12/81
CONT	GRUPO CONTINENTAL, S.A.	INDUSTRIAL GROUP	ORD.	5/79	12/81
CREM	BANCA CREMI	FINANCE	ORD.	4/79	12/81
CRIS	COMPANIA INDUSTRIAL DE SAN CRISTOBAL, S.A.	PAPER AND ALLIED PROD.	A	1/72	12/81
DIAN	EDITORIAL DIANA, S.A	NONDURABLE GOODS	B	1/72	12/78
			ORD.	1/79	12/81
DOMI	DOMINCIA, S.A. DE C.V.	MINING	A*	7/78	12/81

TABLE III.1 (CONTINUED)

****

SECURITY I.D. CODE	NAME OF THE FIRM	TYPE OF OPERATION	SERIES	PERIOD FROM	TO
EATO	EATON MANUFACTURERA, S. A.	AUTOPARTS	A A*	1/72 1/80	12/79 12/81
ECAT	ACEROS ECATEPEC, S.A.	METAL INDUSTRY	ORD. A ORD.	1/72 1/75 1/76	12/74 12/75 12/81
EPEN	EQUIPOS PETROLEROS NACIONALES, S.A.	METAL INDUSTRY	A	9/78	12/81
ERIC	TELEINDUSTRIA ERICSON, S.A.	ELECTRICAL EQUIPMENT	A ORD.	11/76 1/77	12/76 12/81
FRIS	MINERA FRISCO S.A. DE C. V.	MINING	A*	1/72	12/81
FUND	FUNDIDORA MONTERREY,S.A.	METAL INDUSTRY	ORD.	1/72	12/81
GESA	GENERAL ELECTRIC DE MEXICO, S.A.	ELECTRICAL EQUIPMENT	B B*	1/72 6/81	5/81 12/81

****

TABLE III.1 (CONTINUED)

SECURITY I.D. CODE	NAME OF THE FIRM	TYPE OF OPERATION	SERIES	PERIOD FROM	TO
GISS	GRUPO INDUSTRIAL SALTILLO, S.A.	METAL INDUSTRY	B	1/77	12/81
GPOM	GRUPO MEXICO	MINING	A*	8/74	12/78
			A*	1/80	12/81
HOOK	QUIMICA HOOKER, S.A.	CHEMICALS	A	3/77	12/81
HULC	HULERA EL CENTERIO, S.A.	CHEMICALS	A	6/78	12/81
IEM	I.E.M., S.A.	ELECTRICAL EQUIPMENT	ORD.	1/72	3/74
			A	4/74	12/81
IESA	INDUSTRIA ELECTRICA,S.A.	ELECTRICAL EQUIPMENT	ORD.	7/78	12/81
INDE	INDUSTRIA DE TELECOMICACION, S.A.	ELECTRICAL EQUIPMENT	A	1/72	12/79
			A*	1/80	4/81
			*	5/81	12/81
IRSA	INDUSTRIAS RESISTOL,S.A.	CHEMICALS	A*	5/72	12/81
ITEN	BANCO INTERNACIONAL,S.A.	FINANCE	ORD.	1/79	12/81
JDEE	JOHN DEERE, S.A.	AUTOPARTS	A	11/77	5/81
			A*	6/81	12/81
KELS	KELSEY HAYNES, S.A.	AUTOPARTS	A*	11/78	12/81

TABLE III.1 (CONTINUED)

****

SECURITY I.D. CODE	NAME OF THE FIRM	TYPE OF OPERATION	SERIES	PERIOD FROM	PERIOD TO
KIMB	KIMBERLY CLARK DE MEXICO, S.A.	PAPER AND ALLIED PROD.	ORD.	1/72	6/74
			A	7/74	5/81
			A*	6/81	12/81
LAMO	LADRILLERA MONTERREY, S.A.	CONSTRUCTION	ORD.	1/72	12/81
LIVE	EL PUERTO DE LIVERPOOL, S.A.	RETAIL TRADE	ORD.	1/72	12/81
LORE	FABRICAS DE PAPEL LORETO Y PENA POBRE,S.A.	PAPER AND ALLIED PROD.	ORD.	1/72	9/75
			A*	10/75	12/81
LUIS	MINAS DE SAN LUIS, S.A.	MINING	A	1/72	2/74
			A*	3/74	12/77
			A*CP	1/78	5/78
			A*CPN	6/78	12/78
			A*	1/79	12/79
			A*CP	1/80	4/80
			A*	5/80	12/81
MARN	INDUSTRIAS MARTIN, S.A.	NONDURABLE GOODS	A	11/80	12/81

****

TABLE III.1 (CONTINUED)

****

SECURITY I.D. CODE	NAME OF THE FIRM	TYPE OF OPERATION	SERIES	PERIOD FROM	PERIOD TO
MART	MARTELL DE MEXICO, S.A.	NONDURABLE GOODS	ORD.	10/75	12/81
META	METALVER, S.A.	METAL INDUSTRY	A	8/78	12/81
MODE	EMPRESAS LA MODERNA,S.A.	NONDURABLE GOODS	ORD.	1/72	3/74
			A*	4/74	12/81
NEGR	NEGROMEX, S.A.	CHEMICALS	A	1/72	3/74
			A*	4/74	12/81
PALA	EL PALACIO DE HIERRO, S.A.	RETAIL TRADE	ORD.	1/72	12/81
PARI	PARIS-LONDRES, S.A.	RETAIL TRADE	ORD.	10/72	10/81
			A	11/81	12/81
PARR	COMPANIA INDUSTRIAL DEL PARRAS, S.A.	MINING	ORD.	10/80	12/81
PENO	INDUSTRIAS PENOLES, S.A.	MINING	A*	1/72	12/81
PENW	QUIMICA PENWALT, S.A.	CHEMICALS	A*	4/79	12/81
PERK	MOTORES PERKINS, S.A.	AUTOPARTS	A*	6/80	12/81
PETR	PETROCEL, S.A.	CHEMICALS	A*	6/75	12/81
POPO	GENERAL POPO, S.A.	CHEMICALS	ORD.	2/79	12/81

****

TABLE III.1 (CONTINUED)

SECURITY I.D. CODE	NAME OF THE FIRM	TYPE OF OPERATION	SERIES	PERIOD FROM	TO
PURN	INDUSTRIAS PURINA, S.A.	NONDURABLE GOODS	A*	7/78	12/81
PURT	PURITAN, S.A.	NONDURABLE GOODS	ORD.	8/76	12/81
REYN	REYNOLDS ALUMINIO, S.A.	METAL INDUSTRY	ORD.	1/78	12/81
ROBE	ORGANIZACION ROBERT'S, S.A.	RETAIL TRADE	A A*	6/78 1/79	12/78 12/81
SANB	SANBORNS HERMANOS, S.A.	RETAIL TRADE	ORD. A ORD.	1/72 12/77 1/80	11/77 12/79 12/81
SELM	SOCIEDAD ELECTRO MECANICA, S.A.	ELECTRICAL EQUIPMENT	ORD.	1/78	12/81
SPIC	SPICER, S.A.	AUTOPARTS	A*	1/72	12/81
SUDI	SUPER DIESEL, S.A.	AUTOPARTS	B	8/76	12/79
SYR	SALINAS Y ROCHA, S.A	RETAIL TRADE	A* ORD.	1/80 3/81	12/81 12/81

TABLE III.1 (CONTINUED)

SECURITY I.D. CODE	NAME OF THE FIRM	TYPE OF OPERATION	SERIES	PERIOD FROM	PERIOD TO
TAMS	TUBOS DE ACERO DE MEXICO, S.A.	METAL INDUSTRY	A	1/72	5/77
			ORD.	6/77	12/81
TEXA	TEXACO MEXICANA, S.A.	AUTOPARTS	A*	1/79	12/81
TOLT	EMPRESA TOLTECA DE MEXICO, S.A.	CONSTRUCTION	A*	2/72	12/76
TOLM	EMPRESA TOLTECA DE MEXICO, S.A.	CONSTRUCTION	A	1/77	12/81
TREM	TRANSMISIONES Y EQUIPOS MECANICOS, S.A.	AUTOPARTS	A*	1/72	12/81
TUAC	TUBACERO, S.A.	METAL INDUSTRY	ORD.	4/79	12/81
VIRR	EMPRESA VILLAREAL, S.A.	REATIL TRADE	ORD.	8/78	12/81
VISA	VALORES INDUSTRIALES, S.A.	INDUSTRIAL GROUP	A	9/78	12/79
			ORD.	1/80	12/81

TABLE III.1 (CONTINUED)

****

SECURITY I.D. CODE	NAME OF THE FIRM	TYPE OF OPERATION	SERIES	PERIOD FROM	PERIOD TO

****

VITR	VITRO, S.A.	INDUSTRIAL GROUP	ORD.	1/79	12/79
			AA	4/80	4/81
			ORD.	5/81	12/81

****

TABLE III.2

STOCK DATA DETAILS FOR MONTHLY RETURNS

****

SECURITY I.D. CODE	NAME OF THE FIRM	TYPE OF OPERATION	SERIES	PERIOD FROM	TO
ACEY	FUNDIDORA DE ACEROS TEPEYAC, S.A.	METAL INDUSTRY	ORD.	1/72	12/81
ALUM	ALUMINIO, S.A.	METAL INDUSTRY	A*	1/72	12/81
APAS	CEMENTOS APASCO, S.A.	CONSTRUCTION	A	1/72	12/81
AVIA	COMPANIA MEXICANA DE AVIACION, S.A.	SERVICES	ORD.	1/72	12/73
			*	1/74	12/81
BACA	BACARDI Y COMPANIA, S.A.	NONDURABLE GOODS	*	1/72	12/81
BANA	BANAMEX, S.A.	FINANCE	ORD.	1/72	12/81
BCH	BANCO DE CEDULAS HIPOTECARIAS, S.A.	FINANCE	ORD.	1/72	12/81
CAMP	CAMPOS HERMANOS S.A.	METAL INDUSTRY	ORD.	1/72	12/81
CANN	CANNON MILLS. S.A.	NONDURABLE GOODS	ORD.	1/72	5/81
			*	6/81	12/81

****

TABLE III.2 (CONTINUED)

SECURITY I.D. CODE	NAME OF THE FIRM	TYPE OF OPERATION	SERIES	PERIOD FROM	TO
CARB	UNION CARBIDE MEXICANA, S.A	CHEMICALS	A	1/72	12/76
			A*	1/77	12/81
CELA	CELANESE MEXICANA, S.A.	CHEMICALS	A*	1/72	12/81
CENM	CENTRAL DE MALTA, S.A.	NONDURABLE GOODS	ORD.	1/72	12/81
CERM	CERVECERIA MOCTEZUMA, S.A.	NONDURABLE GOODS	ORD.	1/72	12/81
CRIS	COMPANIA INDUSTRIAL DE SAN CRISTOBAL, S.A.	PAPER AND ALLIED PROD.	A	1/72	12/81
DIAN	EDITORIAL DIANA, S.A	NONDURABLE GOODS	B	1/72	12/78
			ORD.	1/79	12/81
EATO	EATON MANUFACTURERA, S. A.	AUTOPARTS	A	1/72	12/79
			A*	1/80	12/81
ECAT	ACEROS ECATEPEC, S.A.	METAL INDUSTRY	ORD.	1/72	12/74
			A	1/75	12/75
			ORD.	1/76	12/81

TABLE III.2 (CONTINUED)

SECURITY I.D. CODE	NAME OF THE FIRM	TYPE OF OPERATION	SERIES	PERIOD FROM	TO
FRIS	MINERA FRISCO S.A. DE C. V.	MINING	A*	1/72	12/81
FUND	FUNDIDORA MONTERREY, S.A.	METAL INDUSTRY	ORD.	1/72	12/81
GESA	GENERAL ELECTRIC DE MEXICO, S.A.	ELECTRICAL EQUIPMENT	B	1/72	5/81
			B*	6/81	12/81
IEM	I.E.M., S.A.	ELECTRICAL EQUIPMENT	ORD.	1/72	3/74
			A	4/74	12/81
INDE	INDUSTRIA DE TELECOMICACION, S.A.	ELECTRICAL EQUIPMENT	A	1/72	12/79
			A*	1/80	4/81
			*	5/81	12/81
KIMB	KIMBERLY CLARK DE MEXICO, S.A.	PAPER AND ALLIED PROD.	ORD.	1/72	6/74
			A	7/74	5/81
			A*	6/81	12/81
LAMO	LADRILLERA MONTERREY, S.A.	CONSTRUCTION	ORD.	1/72	12/81

TABLE III.2 (CONTINUED)

SECURITY I.D. CODE	NAME OF THE FIRM	TYPE OF OPERATION	SERIES	PERIOD FROM	PERIOD TO
LIVE	EL PUERTO DE LIVERPOOL, S.A.	RETAIL TRADE	ORD.	1/72	12/81
LORE	FABRICAS DE PAPEL LORETO Y PENA POBRE,S.A.	PAPER AND ALLIED PROD.	ORD.	1/72	9/75
			A*	10/75	12/81
LUIS	MINAS DE SAN LUIS, S.A.	MINING	A	1/72	2/74
			A*	3/74	12/77
			A*CP	1/78	5/78
			A*CPN	6/78	12/78
			A*	1/79	12/79
			A*CP	1/80	4/80
			A*	5/80	12/81
MODE	EMPRESAS LA MODERNA,S.A.	NONDURABLE GOODS	ORD.	1/72	3/74
			A*	4/74	12/81
MORE	MOTORES Y REFACCIONES, S.A.	AUTOPARTS	A*	1/72	7/74
			A	8/74	12/81
NAFI	NACIONAL FINANCIERA,S.A.	FINANCE	B	1/72	12/81

TABLE III.2 (CONTINUED)

```
**********************************************************************
```

SECURITY I.D. CODE	NAME OF THE FIRM	TYPE OF OPERATION	SERIES	PERIOD FROM	TO
NEGR	NEGROMEX, S.A.	CHEMICALS	A	1/72	3/74
			A*	4/74	12/81
PALA	EL PALACIO DE HIERRO, S.A.	RETAIL TRADE	ORD.	1/72	12/81
PENO	INDUSTRIAS PENOLES, S.A.	MINING	A*	1/72	12/81
SANB	SANBORNS HERMANOS, S.A.	RETAIL TRADE	ORD.	1/72	11/77
			A	12/77	12/79
			ORD.	1/80	12/81
SPIC	SPICER, S.A.	AUTOPARTS	A*	1/72	12/81
TAMS	TUBOS DE ACERO DE MEXICO, S.A.	METAL INDUSTRY	A	1/72	5/77
			ORD.	6/77	12/81
TREM	TRANSMISIONES Y EQUIPOS MECANICOS, S.A.	AUTOPARTS	A*	1/72	12/81
			AA	4/80	4/81
			ORD.	5/81	12/81

```
**********************************************************************
```

TABLE III.3

STOCKS USED TO CALCULATE
THE OLD STOCK PRICE INDEX*

AHMSA	CENM	LORE
ALUM	CERM	MODE
APAS	EATO	PALA
AVIA	ECAT	PARI
CAMP	FRIS	PENO
CANA	FUND	SPIC
CANN	IEM	TAMS
CARB	IRSA	TOLT
CECH	KIMB	TELMEX A
CELA	LIVE	

****

* This list was given by Jorge Lara who is in charge of the department of fundamental analysis at Operadora de Bolsa S.A.

TABLE III.4

SAMPLE OF STOCKS FORMING THE INDEX
July-August 1991

ALFA	*A	CIFRA	*CCP	KIMBER	*A
APASCO	*A	CMA	*CP	LIVEPOL	*2
BACOMER	*BNVO	CODUMEX	*A	MASECA	*A2
BANAMEX	*B	COMERCI	*B2CP	MASECA	*B2
BANORO	*B	COMERMEX	*BNVO	PEÑOLES	*A2
BANORTE	*BNVO	CONTAL		SAN LUIS	*A2
BIMBO	*1	CYDSASA	*A	SERFIN	*B
BIMBO	*2	DESC	*B	TAMSA	*RES
CBACCI		ERICSON	*B	TELMEX	*A
CELANES		FEMSA	*B	TELMEX	*L
CEMEX	*A	GCARSO	*A2NVO	TTOLMEX	*B2
CEMEX	*A	GMEXICO	*A1	VITRO	*NVO
CIFRA	*ACP	GMEXICO	*A2		
CIFRA	*BCP	INTENAL	*B		

TABLE III.5

STATISTICS REGARDING THE DISTRIBUTION OF WEEKLY
RETURNS FOR 34 MEXICAN STOCKS
1972-1981

****

Stock	Ri			Ln(1 + Ri)		
	Mean	Range	St.Dev.	Skewness*	Kurtosis**	Studentized Range
ACCO	.005	0.681	.054	0.269	15.471	13.286&
ACEY	.006	0.697	.073	0.283	4.535	9.832&
ALUM	.004	0.596	.056	0.582	5.310	10.369&
APAS	.008	0.914	.067	-0.788	17.819	14.643&
AVIA	.009	1.046	.080	-0.102@	11.932	13.231&
BACA	.004	0.616	.072	0.951	4.398	8.065&
BANA	.006	0.866	.058	0.377	24.074	15.442&
BIME	.006	2.146	.115	3.099	34.662	15.998&
CAMP	.003	0.866	.091	0.012@	6.712	10.498&
CANN	.012	3.234	.135	4.536	92.964	23.350&
CARB	.005	0.810	.064	-0.817	14.720	13.838&
CELA	.005	1.079	.067	-1.060	30.172	16.174&
CENM	.003	0.790	.054	-2.004	27.009	15.424&
CERM	.004	0.836	.058	-1.219	22.956	15.582&
CRIS	.005	0.938	.062	-1.422	21.067	14.835&

TABLE III.5 (CONTINUED)

****

	Ri			Ln(1 + Ri)		
Stock	Mean	Range	St.Dev.	Skewness*	Kurtosis**	Studentized Range
EATO	.008	0.709	.070	0.565	5.069	9.887&
ECAT	.003	0.935	.081	0.164@	6.910	11.685&
FRIS	.007	0.663	.068	0.435	5.340	9.392&
FUND	.002	1.300	.094	1.536	11.760	11.839&
GESA	.003	0.661	.046	-1.783	22.357	14.604&
IEM	.003	0.880	.075	-0.235	8.105	11.354&
INDE	.007	0.546	.050	0.987	8.783	10.721&
KIMB	.008	1.895	.082	-1.799	70.835	22.852&
LAMO	.005	0.529	.043	-0.084@	16.980	13.060&
LIVE	.005	0.918	.060	-1.965	35.704	16.954&
LORE	.004	0.927	.069	-0.375	15.696	13.878&
LUIS	.010	1.491	.079	-9.492	168.983	22.220&
NEGR	.006	0.479	.040	0.313	14.167	12.411&
PALA	.006	0.603	.047	-0.417	13.869	13.438&
PENO	.010	1.364	.086	1.462	19.178	14.832&
SANB	.007	0.530	.052	0.709	6.373	10.197&
SPIC	.007	0.514	.051	0.560	5.079	10.309&
TAMS	.008	0.784	.073	1.128	5.625	9.747&

TABLE III.5 (CONTINUED)

Stock	Ri			Ln(1 + Ri)		
	Mean	Range	St.Dev.	Skewness*	Kurtosis**	Studentized Range
TREM	.004	0.794	.062	0.546	9.046	12.109&
AVG.	.0058	0.9599	.0686	-0.148	23.048	

The basis of reference is the normal curve which has zero skewness and zero kurtosis.

* Skewness is measured based on the third moment using the following formula:

$$\text{Skewness} = \sum_{i=1}^{N} \frac{((X_i - \overline{X}) / S_x)^3}{N}$$

TABLE III.5 (CONTINUED)

** Kurtosis is measured based on the fourth moment using the following formula:

$$\text{Kurtosis} = \sum_{i=1}^{N} \frac{((X_i - \overline{X}) / S_x)^4}{N} - 3$$

@ Within a two-standard error bound. The standard error for the skewness coefficient is 0.107. The standard error for the kurtosis coefficient is 0.214.

& Exceeds the 0.95 fractile of the distribution of the studentized range(6.94 in samples of size = 500). Therefore, the hypothesis that the return series is normally distributed is rejected and conclude instead that the sample came from a distribution that is "fat-tailed" relative to a normal distribution.

TABLE III.6

STATISTICS REGARDING THE DISTRIBUTION OF WEEKLY
RETURNS FOR 34 MEXICAN STOCKS
SUBPERIOD 1
1972-1976

****

| | Ri | | | Ln(1 + Ri) | | |
Stock	Mean	Range	St.Dev.	Skewness	Kurtosis	Studentized Range
ACCO	.006	0.665	.049	-0.838	25.781	14.162&
ACEY	.008	0.544	.059	1.738	8.454	8.960&
ALUM	.002	0.517	.049	-0.558	7.415	10.594&
APAS	.002	0.480	.039	-0.799	14.186	12.358&
AVIA	.009	1.000	.077	-1.086	18.311	12.892&
BACA	-.001	0.373	.047	0.118@	3.577	7.833&
BANA	.005	0.239	.031	0.725	2.196	7.617&
BIME	-.002	0.807	.083	-0.220@	9.248	9.802&
CAMP	.003	0.837	.097	-0.474	7.883	9.540&
CANN	.010	3.234	.178	5.266	91.039	19.515&
CARB	.003	0.607	.059	0.813	7.070	10.134&
CELA	.002	0.309	.035	-0.058@	4.911	9.073&
CENM	.002	0.372	.034	-0.385	11.362	10.766&
CERM	.002	0.294	.032	0.864	5.867	9.106&

TABLE III.6 (CONTINUED)

****

	Ri			Ln(1 + Ri)		
Stock	Mean	Range	St.Dev.	Skewness	Kurtosis	Studentized Range
CRIS	.000	0.324	.032	-1.500	12.014	10.249&
EATO	.001	0.560	.059	-0.175@	4.688	9.347&
ECAT	.001	0.735	.079	-0.607	7.304	9.913&
FRIS	.007	0.484	.046	-0.217@	8.181	10.724&
FUND	-.001	0.381	.048	-0.398	3.473	8.007&
GESA	.003	0.661	.045	-2.224	36.152	15.049&
IEM	.001	0.320	.043	0.275@	3.093	7.458&
INDE	.007	0.453	.049	1.379	6.692	8.883&
KIMB	.006	0.808	.054	-2.607	35.240	15.297&
LAMO	.005	0.519	.038	-1.020	29.649	14.348&
LIVE	.005	0.649	.047	1.356	24.514	13.604&
LORE	.002	0.315	.031	-0.405	7.500	10.395&
LUIS	.008	0.850	.068	3.071	22.114	11.808&
NEGR	.004	0.476	.033	-0.401	23.356	14.560&
PALA	.006	0.190	.028	0.948	3.488	6.827&
PENO	.007	0.872	.071	1.206	15.439	11.867&
SANB	.005	0.456	.041	1.541	12.245	11.233&
SPIC	.005	0.381	.042	1.486	7.056	8.678&

****

TABLE III.6 (CONTINUED)

****

	Ri			Ln(1 + Ri)		
Stock	Mean	Range	St.Dev.	Skewness	Kurtosis	Studentized Range
****
| TAMS | .002 | 0.431 | .050 | 0.333 | 4.152 | 8.552& |
| TREM | .002 | 0.380 | .038 | 0.093@ | 12.310 | 9.952& |
****
| AVG. | .0037 | 0.603 | .0532 | 0.2456 | 14.597 | |
****

& Exceeds the 0.95 fractile of the distribution of the studentized range (6.38 in samples of size = 200). Therefore, the hypothesis that the return series is normally distributed is rejected.

@ Within a two-standard error bound (st. error = 0.151)

TABLE III.7

STATISTICS REGARDING THE DISTRIBUTIONS OF WEEKLY
RETURNS FOR 34 MEXICAN STOCKS
SUBPERIOD 2
1977-1981

****

Stock	Ri			Ln(1 + Ri)		
	Mean	Range	St.Dev.	Skewness	Kurtosis	Studentized Range
ACCO	.004	0.577	.059	0.983	9.280	9.831&
ACEY	.003	0.587	.084	-0.090@	2.492	7.372&
ALUM	.006	0.549	.063	0.550	3.849	8.387&
APAS	.014	0.914	.086	-0.788	11.628	11.393&
AVIA	.008	0.830	.082	0.861	5.705	9.138&
BACA	.009	0.616	.090	0.884	2.499	6.506&
BANA	.007	0.866	.076	0.286@	15.439	11.827&
BIME	.015	1.993	.138	4.930	44.170	12.628&
CAMP	.003	0.670	.086	0.792	3.743	7.749&
CANN	.014	0.411	.070	0.471	1.148	5.799
CARB	.006	0.770	.068	-1.686	17.099	12.196&
CELA	.008	1.079	.088	-0.965	19.117	12.317&
CENM	.004	0.790	.068	-1.908	19.118	12.128&
CERM	.005	0.836	.076	-1.151	14.281	11.875&

TABLE III.7 (CONTINUED)

****

	Ri			Ln(1 + Ri)		
Stock	Mean	Range	St.Dev.	Skewness	Kurtosis	Studentized Range
CRIS	.009	0.939	.082	-1.250	12.811	11.269&
EATO	.015	0.709	.078	0.835	4.451	8.976&
ECAT	.004	0.781	.083	0.939	6.326	8.869&
FRIS	.007	0.644	.085	0.519	3.084	7.306&
FUND	.006	1.300	.124	1.428	7.171	9.133&
GESA	.002	0.446	.048	-1.399	11.248	9.792&
IEM	.006	0.880	.098	-0.252@	4.654	8.765&
INDE	.006	0.546	.050	0.632	10.459	10.528&
KIMB	.009	1.895	.103	-1.432	60.431	18.867&
LAMO	.006	0.456	.047	0.423	10.055	9.843&
LIVE	.005	0.844	.070	-2.482	29.131	13.277&
LORE	.006	0.927	.093	-0.301@	8.421	10.352&
LUIS	.011	1.266	.089	-9.279	122.545	16.208&
NEGR	.007	0.436	.045	0.564	9.516	9.720&
PALA	.006	0.603	.060	-0.462	9.030	10.456&
PENO	.013	1.364	.098	1.483	18.237	13.154&
SANB	.008	0.530	.061	0.410	3.736	8.603&
SPIC	.009	0.486	.058	0.156	3.608	8.562&

TABLE III.7 (CONTINUED)

****

| | Ri | | | Ln(1 + Ri) | | |
Stock	Mean	Range	St.Dev.	Skewness	Kurtosis	Studentized Range
TAMS	.014	0.776	.090	1.069	3.764	7.910&
TREM	.007	0.794	.079	0.488	5.386	9.564&
AVG.	.0077	0.824	.07868	-0.1394	15.106	

****

& Exceeds the 0.95 fractile of the distribution of the studentized range(6.38 in samples size of = 200). Therefore, the hypothesis that the return series is normally distributed is rejected and conclude instead that the sample came from a distribution that is "fat-tailed" relative to a normal distribution.

@ Within a two-standard error bound. (st. error = 0.151)

TABLE III.8

STATISTICS REGARDING THE DISTRIBUTION OF
WEEKLY PORTFOLIO RETURNS
1972-1981

****

| Port | # Of Sec. | Ri | | | Ln(1 + Ri) | | | |
		Mean	Range	St.Dev.	Skewness	Kurtosis	Studentized Range
Port .1	6	.007	0.552	.040	2.072	16.791	12.795&
Port 2	7	.005	0.351	.030	0.423	6.857	11.870&
Port 3	7	.005	0.362	.033	1.326	7.389	10.452&
Port 4	7	.006	0.302	-.037	0.982	3.877	8.141&
Port 5	7	.006	0.508	.037	0.914	11.444	13.646&

****

E. W. P.	34	.006	0.262	.026	1.074	5.560	9.728&
Market Index	29	.004	0.306	.030			

****

CORR. COEF. (EWP,MI) = 0.83351

& Exceeds the 0.95 fractile of the distribution of the studentized range (6.94 in samples of size=500). Therefore, the hypothesis that the return series is normally distributed is rejected and conclude instead that the sample came from a distribution that is "fat-tailed" relative to a normal distribution.

TABLE III.9

STATISTICS REGARDING THE DISTRIBUTION OF MONTHLY
RETURNS FOR 37 MEXICAN STOCKS

1972-1981

****

	Ri			Ln(1 + Ri)		
Stock	Mean	Range	St.Dev.	Skewness*	Kurtosis**	Studentized Range

****

Stock	Mean	Range	St.Dev.	Skewness*	Kurtosis**	Studentized Range
ACEY	.021	1.058	.164	0.007@	1.535	6.564&
ALUM	.018	0.785	.112	0.055@	2.692	5.115
APAS	.035	1.340	.153	-0.099@	5.979	8.919&
AVIA	.040	1.033	.159	0.152@	1.416	6.328&
BACA	.018	0.994	.154	0.955	1.816	6.190&
BANA	.025	0.786	.099	-0.007@	3.639	8.042&
BCH	.025	1.093	.142	-0.326@	4.980	7.920&
CAMP	.014	1.367	.192	-0.955	6.703	8.111&
CANN	.042	1.316	.164	1.146	3.923	7.081&
CARB	.016	0.723	.107	-0.377@	2.082	6.839&
CELA	.016	0.832	.100	1.072	4.632	7.928&
CENM	.012	0.699	.100	-0.339@	2.966	7.228&
CERM	.017	1.251	.131	-1.635	12.576	9.973&
CRIS	.021	0.906	.136	-0.252@	1.882	6.481&
DIAN	.028	2.791	.238	-1.915	20.029	11.392&

TABLE III.9 (CONTINUED)

****

Stock	Ri			Ln(1 + Ri)		
	Mean	Range	St.Dev.	Skewness*	Kurtosis**	Studentized Range
EATO	.030	0.953	.145	-0.023@	1.324	6.737&
ECAT	.014	1.271	.188	0.407@	1.498	6.744&
FRIS	.025	0.934	.137	-0.253@	1.692	6.956&
FUND	.004	0.932	.141	0.096@	2.166	6.892&
GESA	.014	0.868	.114	-1.035	5.531	7.954&
IEM	.014	0.872	.152	0.344@	1.013	5.614
INDE	.027	0.919	.132	-1.608	8.683	7.997&
KIMB	.032	0.956	.130	0.356@	2.982	7.065&
LAMO	.025	0.848	.111	-0.240@	4.609	7.860&
LIVE	.019	0.524	.084	-0.081@	0.531#	6.156&
LORE	.012	1.650	.159	-0.997	12.002	10.345&
LUIS	.043	0.792	.137	0.288@	0.587#	5.644
MODE	.013	0.874	.129	-0.244@	2.674	7.069&
MORE	.033	0.753	.128	-0.213@	0.676#	5.734
NAFI	.013	0.623	.080	0.993	4.568	7.563&
NEGR	.022	0.516	.074	0.012@	3.041	7.123&
PALA	.025	0.600	.089	-0.307@	2.840	6.925&
PENO	.030	0.869	.134	-0.481	1.531	6.585&

TABLE III.9 (CONTINUED)

****

Stock	Ri			Ln(1 + Ri)		
	Mean	Range	St.Dev.	Skewness*	Kurtosis**	Studentized Range
SANB	.022	0.922	.107	-2.698	21.727	9.797&
SPIC	.032	0.692	.106	0.381@	1.797	6.591&
TAMS	.037	0.753	.118	0.568	1.930	6.215&
TREM	.019	0.952	.135	-0.169@	3.150	7.424&
AVG.	.0230	0.9742	.1273	-0.2005	4.416	

****

The basis of reference is the normal curve which has zero skewness and kurtosis.

* Skewness is measued based on the third moment using the following formula:

$$\text{Skewness} = \sum_{i=1}^{N} \frac{((X_i - \overline{X}) / S_x)^3}{N}$$

TABLE III.9 (CONTINUED)

** Kurtosis is measured based on the fourth moment using the following formula:

$$\text{Kurtosis} = \sum_{i=1}^{N} \frac{((Xi - \overline{X}) / Sx)^4}{N} - 3$$

@ Within a two-standard error bound. The standard error for the skewness coefficient is 0.221.
# Within a two-standard error bound. The standard error for the kurtosis coefficient is 0.438.
& Exceeds the 0.95 fractile of the distribution of the studentized range (5.90 in samples of size = 100). Therefore, the hypothesis that the return series is normally distributed is rejected and conclude instead that the sample came from a distribution that is "fat-tailed" relative to a normal.

TABLE III.10

STATISTICS REGARDING THE DISTRIBUTION OF MONTHLY
RETURNS FOR 37 MEXICAN STOCKS
1972-1976

****

| | Ri | | | Ln(1 + Ri) | | |
Stock	Mean	Range	St.Dev.	Skewness*	Kurtosis**	Studentized Range
ACEY	.035	0.639	.133	0.624	0.135#	4.852
ALUM	.010	0.730	.106	0.582@	3.636	6.908&
APAS	.008	0.340	.064	-0.384@	1.133#	5.494
AVIA	.049	0.987	.169	0.809	2.271	5.8677&
BACA	-.005	0.477	.087	-0.033@	0.433#	5.439
BANA	.023	0.438	.071	0.572@	1.880	6.206&
BCH	.014	0.342	.069	-0.246@	0.078#	4.979
CAMP	.005	1.367	.206	-1.444	7.018	7.131&
CANN	.025	1.316	.171	2.192	10.191	7.287&
CARB	.014	0.723	.116	-0.437@	3.123	6.306&
CELA	.008	0.346	.058	0.722	1.950	5.881&
CENM	.009	0.345	.062	0.437@	0.871#	5.420
CERM	.009	0.425	.076	0.437@	1.288	5.602&
CRIS	.002	0.437	.070	-1.554	6.015	6.490&
DIAN	.049	2.663	.285	0.445@	19.213	10.139&

TABLE III.10 (CONTINUED)

****

	Ri			Ln(1 + Ri)		
Stock	Mean	Range	St.Dev.	Skewness*	Kurtosis**	Studentized Range
EATO	-.000	0.804	.122	-0.785	3.059	6.665&
ECAT	-.005	1.104	.176	-0.030@	1.381	6.247&
FRIS	.029	0.455	.096	0.169@	0.196#	4.844
FUND	-.006	0.521	.083	0.001@	2.272	6.172&
GESA	.014	0.559	.081	-1.200	7.341	7.205&
IEM	.004	0.444	.092	0.710	0.678#	4.719
INDE	.033	0.639	.121	0.253@	0.615#	5.475
KIMB	.033	0.699	.113	0.930	2.855	6.109&
LAMO	.022	0.754	.104	-1.139	7.280	7.368&
LIVE	.021	0.412	.068	0.995	2.410	5.819&
LORE	.006	0.312	.055	0.750	0.948#	5.565&
LUIS	.034	0.722	.125	0.837	1.425	5.527&
MODE	-.000	0.852	.110	-1.152	6.983	7.696&
MORE	.023	0.473	.079	0.033@	1.484#	6.029&
NAFI	.012	0.189	.031	0.579@	2.213	6.164&
NEGR	.016	0.267	.054	0.610@	0.350#	4.921
PALA	.025	0.223	.052	-0.095@	-0.347#	4.360
PENO	.026	0.788	.124	0.062@	1.927	6.319&

****

TABLE III.10 (CONTINUED)

****

| | Ri | | | Ln(1 + Ri) | | |
Stock	Mean	Range	St.Dev.	Skewness*	Kurtosis**	Studentized Range
SANB	.024	0.435	.083	1.310	1.906	5.113
SPIC	.023	0.512	.084	1.218	2.830	5.959&
TAMS	.017	0.395	.073	-0.116@	0.700#	5.424
TREM	.006	0.412	.068	-0.174@	1.955	5.943&
AVG.	.0165	0.636	.0967	0.1753	2.7371	

****

& Exceeds the 0.95 fractile of the distribution of the studentized range.
@ Within a two-standard error bound (st. error = 0.309)
# Within a two-standard error bound (st. error = 0.608)

TABLE III.11

STATISTICS REGARDING THE DISTRIBUTION OF MONTHLY
RETURNS FOR 37 MEXICAN STOCKS
1977-1981

Stock	Ri			Ln(1 + Ri)		
	Mean	Range	St.Dev.	Skewness*	Kurtosis**	Studentized Range
ACEY	.006	1.058	.190	-0.0010@	0.998#	5.5933&
ALUM	.025	0.738	.118	-0.3332@	2.044	6.3361&
APAS	.062	1.340	.204	-0.3221@	2.658	6.6811&
AVIA	.031	0.658	.149	-0.5000@	0.156#	4.630
BACA	.041	0.994	.199	0.742	0.219#	4.891
BANA	.026	0.786	.121	-0.102@	2.240	6.5532&
BCH	.037	1.093	.189	-0.3317@	2.052	5.9952&
CAMP	.022	0.960	.179	0.534@	0.865#	5.5368&
CANN	.060	0.709	.156	0.230@	-0.474#	4.410
CARB	.018	0.398	.098	-0.2223@	-0.670#	4.142
CELA	.024	0.832	.129	0.843	2.243	6.177&
CENM	.016	0.699	.127	-0.384@	1.239	5.643&
CERM	.026	1.251	.170	-1.502	7.414	7.592&
CRIS	.039	0.906	.178	-0.276@	0.113#	4.976
DIAN	.007	1.205	.180	-3.452	18.580	7.592&

TABLE 111.11 (CONTINUED)

****

	Ri			Ln(1 + Ri)		
Stock	Mean	Range	St.Dev.	Skewness*	Kurtosis**	Studentized Range
EATO	.061	0.794	.161	0.299@	-0.285#	4.803
ECAT	.032	1.079	.199	0.822	1.179#	5.039
FRIS	.020	0.934	.169	-0.181@	0.597#	5.607&
FUND	.013	0.932	.182	0.044@	0.529#	5.365
GESA	.014	0.868	.140	-0.839	3.276	6.479&
IEM	.023	0.872	.194	0.218@	-0.219#	4.384
INDE	.021	0.882	.143	-2.120	8.811	6.770&
KIMB	.031	0.956	.146	0.129@	2.292	6.209&
LAMO	.028	0.693	.118	0.561@	1.939	5.706&
LIVE	.017	0.407	.098	-0.333@	-0.525#	4.247
LORE	.018	1.650	.219	-0.715	5.255	7.511&
LUIS	.053	0.751	.148	-0.072@	0.051#	4.945
MODE	.027	0.752	.145	0.204@	-0.016#	5.163
MORE	.042	0.753	.164	-0.275@	-0.460#	4.488
NAFI	.015	0.623	.110	0.802	1.393	5.552&
NEGR	.028	0.516	.089	-0.215@	2.128	5.851&
PALA	.025	0.600	.115	-0.221@	1.020#	5.347
PENO	.034	0.710	.144	-0.770	1.048#	5.207

****

TABLE 111.11 (CONTINUED)

****

	Ri			Ln(1 + Ri)		
Stock	Mean	Range	St.Dev.	Skewness*	Kurtosis**	Studentized Range
SANB	.021	0.922	.127	-2.864	16.213	7.809&
SPIC	.040	0.692	.125	0.032@	0.807#	5.544&
TAMS	.057	0.753	.149	0.358@	0.579#	5.008
TREM	.031	0.952	.179	-0.220@	0.939#	5.618&
AVG.	.0294	0.857	.1527	-0.2817	2.302	

****

& Exceeds the 0.95 fractile of the distribution of the studentized range.
@ Within a two-standard error bound (st. error = 0.309)
# Within a two-standard error bound (st. error = 0.608)

TABLE III.12

STATISTICS REGARDING THE DISTRIBUTION OF
MONTHLY PORTFOLIO RETURNS
1972-1981

****

		Ri				Ln(1 + Ri)	
Port	# Of Sec.	Mean	Range	St.Dev.	Skewness	Kurtosis	Studentized Range

****

Port	# Of Sec.	Mean	Range	St.Dev.	Skewness	Kurtosis	Studentized Range
Port. 1	7	.025	0.583	.075	0.006@	3.149	7.876&
Port. 2	7	.022	0.485	.076	0.203@	1.406	6.313&
Port. 3	7	.023	0.422	.080	0.417@	0.476#	5.292
Port. 4	8	.025	0.488	.084	0.560	0.872#	5.675
Port. 5	8	.021	0.448	.070	-0.485	1.851#	6.525&
E. W. P.	37	.023	0.403	.067	0.381@	0.964	5.925

****

& Exceeds the 0.95 fractile of the distribution of the studentized range.
@ Within a two-standard error bound.
# Within a two-standard error bound.

TABLE III.13

STATISTICS REGARDING THE DISTRIBUTION OF
MONTHLY PORTFOLIO RETURNS
1972-1976

****

			Ri		Ln(1 + Ri)			Studentized
Port	# Of Sec.	Mean	Range	St.Dev.	Skewness	Kurtosis		Range

****

Port. 1	7	.015	0.243	.043	1.085	2.769		5.658&
Port. 2	7	.013	0.372	.051	0.674	2.309		6.440&
Port. 3	7	.018	0.292	.054	0.744	1.273		5.317
Port. 4	8	.022	0.370	.072	0.721	1.047#		5.077
Port. 5	8	.015	0.389	.059	0.204@	3.041		6.527&

****

E. W. P.	37	.017	0.288	.047	0.704	2.583		6.120&

****

& Exceeds the 0.95 fractile of the distribution of the studentized range.
@ Within a two-standard error bound.
# Within a two-standard error bound.

TABLE III.14

STATISTICS REGARDING THE DISTRIBUTION OF
MONTHLY PORTFOLIO RETURNS
1977-1981

****

		Ri			Ln(1 + Ri)		
Port	# Of Sec.	Mean	Range	St.Dev.	Skewness	Kurtosis	Studentized Range

****

Port	# Of Sec.	Mean	Range	St.Dev.	Skewness	Kurtosis	Studentized Range
Port. 1	7	.034	0.583	.097	-0.277@	1.123#	6.078&
Port. 2	7	.030	0.485	.094	-0.057@	0.237#	5.077
Port. 3	7	.028	0.422	.100	0.240@	-0.539#	4.229
Port. 4	8	.029	0.488	.095	0.422@	0.383#	5.029
Port. 5	8	.027	0.409	.079	-0.816	1.136#	5.309

****

E. W. P.	37	.029	0.403	.082	0.148@	-0.169#	4.810

****

& Exceeds the 0.95 fractile of the distribution of the studentized range.
@ Within a two-standard error bound.
# Within a two-standard error bound.

TABLE III.15

CORRELATION MATRIX FOR MEXICAN MONTHLY RETURNS

	ACEY	ALUM	APAS	AVIA	BACA	BANA	BCH
ACEY	1.00000						
ALUM	0.12727	1.00000					
APAS	0.15497	0.25451	1.00000				
AVIA	0.20101	0.23438	0.30407	1.00000			
BACA	0.15906	0.30972	0.21344	0.18877	1.00000		
BANA	0.20497	0.26660	0.19749	0.36488	0.23457	1.00000	
BCH	-0.00905	0.17563	0.06280	0.20912	0.33451	0.21849	1.00000
CAMP	0.18956	0.17997	0.24765	0.16198	0.27499	0.36198	0.25347
CANN	0.20593	0.18896	0.35193	0.23974	0.23531	0.24025	0.05822
CARB	0.39116	0.33979	0.27263	0.40637	0.24469	0.43846	0.23647
CELA	0.37221	0.31782	0.55277	0.47464	0.44231	0.32115	0.11764
CENM	0.15348	0.19891	0.30534	0.26793	0.25774	0.28269	0.27625
CERM	0.32592	0.24883	0.51524	0.46289	0.23798	0.32087	0.21696
CRIS	0.15377	0.29815	0.18761	0.33700	0.32083	0.31604	0.19520
DIAN	0.02902	0.13113	0.25745	0.10554	0.20570	0.24070	0.08969
EATO	0.37466	0.24688	0.43686	0.30532	0.34261	0.27544	0.24612
ECAT	0.24183	0.10854	0.27896	0.13812	0.119490	0.30712	-0.06591
FRIS	0.08634	0.02580	0.16059	0.26325	0.12866	0.33719	0.12618
FUND	0.07804	0.29103	0.21258	0.23404	0.37710	0.25996	0.16796
GESA	0.19840	0.12925	0.17435	0.16482	0.27113	0.23213	-0.06674

[TABLE III.15 (CONTINUED)]

	ACEY	ALUM	APAS	AVIA	BACA	BANA	BCH
IEM	0.13874	0.12735	-0.04470	0.15653	0.17256	0.29182	0.16878
INDE	0.17895	0.21245	0.02135	0.29964	0.12857	0.21280	0.22578
KIMB	0.23044	0.28719	0.35118	0.29319	0.29498	0.21131	0.24470
LAMO	0.10855	0.19767	0.36075	0.23794	0.16871	0.19176	-0.04099
LIVE	0.21706	0.29365	0.24733	0.37403	0.24396	0.27279	0.17988
LORE	0.08982	0.07718	0.21294	0.25403	0.25966	0.19895	0.18391
LUIS	0.09696	0.22671	0.15701	0.35204	0.13136	0.21494	0.13569
MODE	0.08773	0.30243	0.35851	0.30037	0.32197	0.37590	0.21918
MORE	0.16913	0.22901	0.29951	0.37664	0.44164	0.15870	0.40536
NAFI	0.22175	0.28355	0.50614	0.33629	0.28163	0.30257	0.23815
NEGR	0.14463	0.22340	0.07710	0.10256	0.10980	0.22381	0.14585
PALA	0.22113	0.26485	0.37955	0.32228	0.27073	0.27409	0.01940
PENO	0.18926	0.16715	0.23888	0.27266	0.11355	0.27716	0.04439
SANB	0.26326	0.30640	0.34294	0.30835	0.27911	0.38189	0.19864
SPIC	0.31152	0.39490	0.39713	0.39746	0.27680	0.38943	0.16192
TAMS	0.14011	0.35163	0.28195	0.13817	0.16362	0.33837	-0.11126
TREM	0.20351	0.11530	0.25602	0.38267	0.07155	0.16582	0.12301

TABLE III.15 (CONTINUED)

	CAMP	CANN	CARB	CELA	CENM	CERM	CRIS
CAMP	1.00000						
CANN	0.17566	1.00000					
CARB	0.29277	0.23522	1.00000				
CELA	0.34410	0.39826	0.53595	1.00000			
CENM	0.27101	0.16654	0.35357	0.34821	1.00000		
CERM	0.29486	0.32853	0.47543	0.73401	0.36833	1.00000	
CRIS	0.18522	0.27525	0.38446	0.56149	0.29818	0.49483	1.00000
DIAN	0.11392	0.04655	0.12675	0.24686	0.20383	0.25398	0.23410
EATO	0.33791	0.37189	0.51143	0.54773	0.37960	0.45363	0.36586
ECAT	0.25855	0.21253	0.28054	0.51964	0.11811	0.43564	0.26474
FRIS	0.32025	0.21097	0.30300	0.32709	0.15087	0.41418	0.31011
FUND	0.24470	0.06307	0.26175	0.34617	0.10818	0.11572	0.10989
GESA	0.13821	0.22107	0.23524	0.36107	0.10820	0.27159	0.23347
IEM	0.08993	0.05072	0.12681	0.15399	0.05159	0.11954	0.13086
INDE	0.21180	0.18499	0.35354	0.24826	0.16777	0.28969	0.24014
KIMB	0.31654	0.17752	0.57146	0.54063	0.46410	0.42448	0.33837
LAMO	0.05903	0.21808	0.30155	0.38792	0.33113	0.34170	0.17402
LIVE	0.11361	0.25880	0.39478	0.47071	0.51635	0.38545	0.28448
LORE	0.24986	0.17444	0.20351	0.41542	0.20313	0.48969	0.32031
LUIS	0.09682	0.13420	0.31515	0.28484	0.17664	0.28616	0.34295
MODE	0.37393	0.29121	0.50239	0.54701	0.40782	0.33026	0.41876
MORE	0.28021	0.10301	0.26114	0.42948	0.48258	0.34375	0.29275

TABLE III.15 (CONTINUED)

	CAMP	CANN	CARB	CELA	CENM	CERM	CRIS
NAFI	0.29082	0.32120	0.34333	0.59754	0.18022	0.58210	0.32389
NEGR	0.21520	0.20294	0.20615	0.13023	0.28634	0.12998	0.26714
PALA	0.32285	0.24610	0.30345	0.35021	0.26919	0.24279	0.13718
PENO	0.21598	0.19935	0.33942	0.35775	0.14643	0.39746	0.24494
SANB	0.32810	0.19229	0.34270	0.35593	0.22514	0.42036	0.31837
SPIC	0.30839	0.30629	0.47288	0.60704	0.25039	0.60523	0.45986
TAMS	0.18982	0.27576	0.24983	0.24761	0.16158	0.17882	0.15014
TREM	0.28599	0.28174	0.32762	0.38104	0.42879	0.28400	0.28730

TABLE III.15 (CONTINUED)

	DIAN	EATO	ECAT	FRIS	FUND	GESA	IEM
DIAN	1.00000						
EATO	0.20313	1.00000					
ECAT	0.09532	0.38531	1.00000				
FRIS	0.12180	0.12380	0.21751	1.00000			
FUND	0.14742	0.21126	0.11580	0.04734	1.00000		
GESA	0.12668	0.34898	0.10623	0.06340	0.10035	1.00000	
IEM	0.05911	0.05406	-0.00043	-0.04414	0.23523	0.25805	1.00000
INDE	0.01410	0.23682	0.04732	0.19786	0.08342	0.19839	0.19895
KIMB	0.18782	0.51952	0.28697	0.26936	0.21295	0.31486	0.01927
LAMO	0.20093	0.21542	0.20788	0.15333	0.07368	0.32758	0.08371
LIVE	0.14540	0.36082	0.19760	0.08217	0.06513	0.16509	0.09233
LORE	0.18553	0.35510	0.27332	0.14081	0.10001	0.33261	0.19649
LUIS	0.18291	0.15791	0.16404	0.28607	0.03668	0.15192	0.09437
MODE	0.14289	0.52552	0.30375	0.29668	0.44017	0.22982	0.11671
MORE	0.11690	0.45429	0.17734	0.12905	0.17015	0.16131	0.13372
NAFI	0.19565	0.31810	0.44715	0.34817	0.14466	0.19540	0.07355
NEGR	0.14970	0.31365	0.15952	0.15375	0.09402	0.21169	0.16985
PALA	0.08310	0.33355	0.24079	0.35350	0.08021	0.28227	0.11437
PENO	0.11924	0.18942	0.27451	0.56349	0.12827	-0.05219	0.10554
SANB	0.21921	0.32666	0.18066	0.20897	0.05734	0.24489	0.16418

TABLE III.15 (CONTINUED)

	DIAN	EATO	ECAT	FRIS	FUND	GESA	IEM
SPIC	0.14179	0.51948	0.39002	0.29474	0.11546	0.39392	0.22114
TAMS	0.08045	0.16975	0.16928	0.22305	0.22373	0.25537	0.16396
TREM	0.11485	0.42645	0.25366	0.21760	0.09364	0.13507	0.15853

	INDE	KIMB	LAMO	LIVE	LORE	LUIS	MODE
INDE	1.00000						
KIMB	0.31639	1.00000					
LAMO	0.18502	0.42198	1.00000				
LIVE	0.20749	0.40978	0.26680	1.00000			
LORE	0.31858	0.28711	0.24945	0.13858	1.00000		
LUIS	0.29544	0.35742	0.24386	0.28483	-0.05298	1.00000	
MODE	0.16973	0.42390	0.27596	0.34333	0.20626	0.06434	1.00000
MORE	0.15849	0.33178	0.20028	0.37982	0.24998	0.19240	0.36967
NAFI	0.09571	0.25058	0.25160	0.25544	0.28291	0.17011	0.33172
NEGR	0.20163	0.14973	0.13796	0.21301	0.14073	0.07206	0.16282
PALA	0.17489	0.29704	0.26768	0.30852	0.17006	0.24853	0.30008
PENO	0.27347	0.27078	0.08937	0.17313	0.11303	0.39444	0.26486
SANB	0.25939	0.44206	0.36354	0.22948	0.43617	0.23146	0.20787
SPIC	0.31462	0.38363	0.43227	0.36187	0.36766	0.30013	0.31950
TAMS	0.22183	0.17272	0.28544	0.12425	0.14956	0.27400	0.19978
TREM	0.28775	0.36799	0.31309	0.47931	0.14679	0.33445	0.34439

TABLE III.15 (CONTINUED)

	MORE	NAFI	NEGR	PALA	PENO	SANB	SPIC
MORE	1.00000						
NAFI	0.33332	1.00000					
NEGR	0.21166	0.29205	1.00000				
PALA	0.30972	0.42392	0.30243	1.00000			
PENO	0.14625	0.27152	0.14698	0.35068	1.00000		
SANB	0.22931	0.19115	0.07991	0.23508	0.25949	1.00000	
SPIC	0.35550	0.46420	0.43082	0.24952	0.24677	0.43853	1.00000
TAMS	0.04942	0.18292	0.11089	0.25728	0.19532	0.32145	0.31687
TREM	0.39643	0.24194	0.34492	0.39996	0.15375	0.07447	0.33204

	TAMS	TREM
TAMS	1.00000	
TREM	0.04791	1.00000

AVERAGE CORRELATION COEFFICIENT = 0.24742

TABLE III.16

THE EFFECTS OF DIVERSIFICATION *

****

# OF SECURITIES IN THE PORTFOLIO	AVERAGE MEAN	AVERAGE STANDARD DEVIATION
1	0.02177	0.15107
2	0.02477	0.10821
3	0.02296	0.09702
4	0.02350	0.09199
5	0.02278	0.08385
6	0.02317	0.08058
7	0.02292	0.07760
8	0.02281	0.07547
9	0.02284	0.07409
10	0.02276	0.07309
11	0.02306	0.07197
12	0.02322	0.07125
13	0.02302	0.07110
14	0.02316	0.07158
15	0.02312	0.07168
16	0.02300	0.07103
17	0.02318	0.07058

****

TABLE III.16 (CONTINUED)

# OF SECURITIES IN THE PORTFOLIO	AVERAGE MEAN	AVERAGE STANDARD DEVIATION
18	0.02303	0.07050
19	0.02302	0.06989
20	0.02289	0.06945
21	0.02285	0.06911
22	0.02274	0.06918
23	0.002292	0.06862
24	0.02286	0.06828
25	0.02287	0.06792
26	0.02278	0.06748
27	0.02291	0.06751
28	0.02302	0.06738
29	0.02297	0.06742
30	0.02310	0.06740
31	0.02317	0.06742
32	0.02322	0.06723
33	0.02325	0.06688

TABLE III.16 (CONTINUED)

****

# OF SECURITIES IN THE PORTFOLIO	AVERAGE MEAN	AVERAGE STANDARD DEVIATION
34	0.02319	0.06654
35	0.02319	0.06664
36	0.02310	0.06662
37	0.02306	0.06673

****

* The securities were selected randomly (drawing without replacement).

TABLE III.17

THE EFFECTS OF EXTENDED HEDGED DIVERSIFICATION *

****

# OF SECURITIES IN THE PORTFOLIO	AVERAGE MEAN	AVERAGE STANDARD DEVIATION
1	0.01037	0.09495
2	0.01314	0.07860
3	0.01369	0.06835
4	0.01398	0.06679
5	0.01533	0.06468
6	0.01495	0.06016
7	0.01551	0.05885
8	0.01596	0.05909
9	0.01609	0.05805
10	0.01567	0.05629
11	0.01578	0.05547
12	0.01565	0.05447
13	0.01560	0.05427
14	0.01567	0.05405
15	0.01566	0.05281
16	0.01575	0.05265
17	0.01569	0.05170
18	0.01579	0.05163

****

TABLE III.17 (CONTINUED)

****

# OF SECURITIES IN THE PORTFOLIO	AVERAGE MEAN	AVERAGE STANDARD DEVIATION
19	0.01593	0.05168
20	0.01591	0.05100
25	0.01594	0.05041
30	0.01579	0.04907
40	0.01640	0.04890
50	0.01644	0.04877
58	0.01648	0.04867

****

* The securities were selected randomly (drawing without replacement).

TABLE III.18

THE EFFECTS OF EXTENDED UNHEDGED DIVERSIFICATION *

****

# OF SECURITIES IN THE PORTFOLIO	AVERAGE MEAN	AVERAGE STANDARD DEVIATION
1	0.01576	0.11037
2	0.01698	0.08866
3	0.01727	0.07423
4	0.01743	0.07092
5	0.01839	0.06685
6	0.01801	0.06328
7	0.01846	0.06184
8	0.01873	0.06102
9	0.01880	0.05990
10	0.01850	0.05850
11	0.01863	0.05742
12	0.01851	0.05640
13	0.01847	0.05585
14	0.01849	0.05511
15	0.01850	0.05393
16	0.01855	0.05361
17	0.01855	0.05279
18	0.01863	0.05269

****

TABLE III.18 (CONTINUED)

****

# OF SECURITIES IN THE PORTFOLIO	AVERAGE MEAN	AVERAGE STANDARD DEVIATION
19	0.01873	0.05275
20	0.01877	0.05218
25	0.01880	0.05132
30	0.01871	0.05022
40	0.01918	0.04977
50	0.01915	0.04930
58	0.01924	0.04928

****

* The securities were selected randomly (drawing without replacement).

TABLE III.19

$$\frac{S1 - S0}{S0}(Mex) = C + B\ R(us) + E$$

R(us)	C	T(C)	B	T(B)	R(us)	C	T(C)	B	T(B)
ALD	0.008	1.323	0.014	0.205	HR	0.008	1.332	-0.059	-0.965
AA	0.008	1.374	-0.014	-0.200	IP	0.008	1.385	-0.023	-0.320
ATT	0.008	1.300	0.015	0.103	OI	0.008	1.391	-0.025	-0.343
BS	0.008	1.399	-0.033	-0.531	PG	0.008	1.360	-0.006	-0.059
CH	0.008	1.341	-0.016	-0.363	S	0.008	1.333	-0.038	-0.447
DD	0.008	1.383	-0.032	-0.407	TX	0.008	1.325	0.018	0.247
EK	0.008	1.402	-0.082	-1.023	UK	0.008	1.417	-0.042	-0.535
GE	0.008	1.356	0.001	0.009	X	0.008	1.370	-0.011	-0.168
GF	0.008	1.364	-0.008	-0.106	WX	0.008	1.344	0.024	0.394
GM	0.008	1.338	0.061	0.674	Z	0.008	1.365	-0.022	-0.338
GT	0.008	1.369	-0.017	- 0.209	E.W.P.	0.008	1.387	-0.038	-0.345

CHAPTER IV

THE EFFICIENCY OF THE MEXICAN STOCK MARKET

One of the most important notions in the field of finance is that capital markets are efficient. Although the concept of efficiency has different meanings in finance, most scholars use it to refer to what Tobin (1984) calls information-arbitrage efficiency. The market is said to be efficient in this sense if the price of a security fully reflects all available "relevant information" and respond rapidly to new information as soon as it becomes available.

The efficient market is a hypothesis about the behavior of certain security, commodity, service or any other item whose price and quantity is determined by supply and demand. As such, it needs to be tested to see how accurately it describes reality. Therefore, it is of interest at both the theoretical and empirical level[19].

The efficient market hypothesis is concerned with those conditions in which investors can use information available at a point in time to make an estimate and earn a return greater than the equilibrium return[20]. The market is said to efficient if there is no way in which investors can use the available "relevant information" to make a profit beyond that which is consistent with the risk inherent in the security[21].

What is the "relevant information"?. There are many pieces of information that can be considered relevant, such as past prices, announcements of earnings and dividends, annual reports, changes in accounting practices, inside information, etc.

---

[19] The efficient market hypothesis was first tested by Kendall (1953). Then, people in academics went in search of a theory to explain the accumulated evidence. This is the opposite to the general procedure in which first a theory is suggested and then tests are performed to see how well it describes actual behavior.

[20] Typically an estimate of the equilibrium return comes out of the Capital Asset Pricing Model (C.A.P.M.) or the Arbitrage Pricing Theory (A.P.T.).

[21] In other words, the market is said to be efficient when the purchase or sale of a security at the prevaling market price is a transaction with a net present value of zero.

114

Most tests try to determined whether prices fully reflects an specific subset of information. Here, I am interested in whether the information contanied in the past sequence of the security price (or return) is fully and instantaneously reflected in its current price. This has been done in sophisticated capital markets of developed countries and most evidence suggests efficiency in this sense[22]. However, one must be careful in interpreting the results of these papers. Such conclusions should be limited to the country of study and the time span used. This is why research in smaller and less sophisticated capital markets like Mexico is very important.

A. SERIAL CORRELATION TESTS ON RETURNS

If the market is efficient in the sense that the current price of a security fully reflects its past sequence of prices; then, one would not expect to find a relationship between the past price change or return series and future price changes or returns. One can never prove the statement that the information contanied in past price changes of one share can not be used to predict its future movements since there is an infinite number of ways that the sequence of past price changes can be used to forecast future price changes. However, one can test particular forms of using past price changes data to predict future price changes.

Several tests of different price patterns have been performed using data on both American and foreing security prices. At present in Mexico, there is only one paper that examines the efficiency of the Mexican stock market. Ortiz (1980) performed a runs test based on monthly prices for 79 shares for the 1967-1979 period[23]. His results showed that there is

---

[22] Nevertheless, some persistent and large irregularities have been detected in these capital markets lately. These irregularities have been called market anomalies. Among them we have : a) the "size effect" in which firms with low total market value of common stock seem to produce excess returns. b) the "January effect" in which stocks seem to produce an excess return the month of January; and c) the "high earning/price effect" in which stocks that sell at high E/P ratio seem to produce excess returns. These anomalies are still a puzzle; investigators do not know whether they are really inefficiencies or it is the product of measuring risk incorrectly or having the wrong equilibrium model.

[23] Ortiz (1980) does not note whether or not the monthly prices are adjusted.

some dependency among price changes. In particular, price changes in one direction tend to be followed by price changes in the same direction. That is, the correlation between two succesive price changes is positive. He indicated that this relationship although statistically significant is not large enough to be important. This suggests that the significant departures from randomness might be so small as to be of no practical importance for those investors who try to obtain abnormal profits.

Although the runs count is not influenced by extreme observations, it is only a diagnostic check for randomness.

This study examines the correlation coefficient between past returns and future returns $p(Rit,Rit-1)$. An estimate of p will tell if the return series follows a random walk. The random walk model states that any price change is independent of the sequence of previous price changes. Market efficiency would then imply that the autocorrelations of the returns on any security are zero for all lags.

A.1. WEEKLY RETURNS

Table IV.1 shows the sample autocorrelation of weekly returns for 91 stocks. The time periods vary from stock to stock but usually run from 1972 to 1981. For each stock, the table shows sample autocorrelations for lags from one to eight weeks. Under the hypothesis that the true autocorrelation is zero, the sample autocorrelation coefficients for lags greater than zero, are approximately distributed according to a normal distribution with mean zero and standard deviation 1/sq. root of the number of observations. Thus, if a stock has 521 observations, one can assign a standard error of .044 to the first autocorrelation coefficient. Then, if the first autocorrelation coefficient was greater than .088, one could be 95% certain that the true autocorrelation coefficient is significantly different from zero.

In Table IV.1, the sample autocorrelations that are at least two standard errors to the left or to the right of zero are indicated by asterisks. At lag one, 28 out of 91 sample autocorrelations are statistically different from zero. Of the 28, 23 are negative. It seems like the market overreacts. These results are consistent with those of Cootner (1962), and Cheng and Deets (1971), who found a preponderance of negative signs for weekly price changes. Fama (1965) analyzed first order serial correlations for nine-day changes on the Dow-Jones industrials. His results show a preponderance of negative coefficients but only 2 out the 30 are statistically different from zero. However, Kendall (1953) found positive serial correlation for weekly returns.

To investigate the stationarity over time of the negative serial correlation for Mexican securities, the 1972-1981 period was subdivided into two five-year subperiods. Table IV.2 shows the sample autocorrelations for the 1972-1976 subperiod and Table IV.3 presents the sample autocorrelation for the 1977-1981 subperiod. From the analysis of these tables one can conclude that the statistical significance of the negative serial correlation was quite consistent over the time under consideration.

The sample autocorrelations for the portfolios described in section III.B are presented in Table IV.4. As one can see from the table, two out of the five portfolios are statistically different from zero at lag one. In contrast with the negative serial correlation found for individual securities, the two significant coefficients are positive. These results provide empirical evidence of the "Fisher effect" in which measured returns deviate from true returns. The "Fisher effect" comes from the fact that reported closing prices typically represent trades prior to the actual close of the trading day. This anomaly in the way the data is collected was pointed out by Fisher (1966) who found that an index constructed from such data suffers from positive serial correlation and its estimated variance is biased downward.

A.2. MONTHLY RETURNS

Table IV.5 shows sample autocorrelations of monthly returns for lags L = 1,2......8, for the 37 stocks not missing an observation over the 1972-1981 period. Seven out of the 37 first order serial correlations are statistically different from zero. Of the seven, four are negative and three are positive.

Tables IV.6 and IV.7 shed some light on the stationarity of the coefficients over two non-overlaping five-year subperiods. Of the seven significant stocks in the overall period, two are not significant in the subperiods.

The sample autocorrelations for portfolios are presented in Tables IV.8, IV.9 and IV.10. Two out of the five portfolios are significant in the 1972-1981 period, but this significance is not consistent over time. It is also important to note that the first-order serial correlation for the equally weighted portfolio as well as the market value portfolio are statistically different from zero in the overall period. This significance is not found in the 1972-1976 subperiod but reappears in the 1977-1978 subperiod.

The results of the serial correlation tests on both weekly and monthly returns on individual shares as well as portfolios seem to indicate some linear dependencies in the period of time analyzed. As far as these tests are concerned the Mexican stock market was weak-form inefficient in the sense that the current prices did not reflect the sequence of past prices over the 1972-1981 period.

A.3. MONTHLY REAL RETURNS

So far, autocorrelation tests have been performed on nominal rates of return; that is, on rates of return that are expressed in units of pesos. However, investors are assumed to be concerned with real rates of return on stocks. Real rates are not expressed in pesos, they are stated in units of purchasing power of a representative bundle of goods and services.

The real rate of return on a security from the end of month t-1 to the end of month t is the nominal return minus the inflation rate over the same period. In equation form:

$$RR_t = R_t - P_t \qquad (4.1)$$

where

RR_t is the real rate of return
R_t is the nominal rate of return and
P_t is the inflation rate as measured by the change of the Consumer Price Index

Actually the nominal rate of return is equal to the real return plus the inflation rate plus the product of the real rate and the inflation rate. However, since the cross-product term was generally small in the 1972-1981 period, it is simpler just to add the inflation rate to the real return to get the nominal rate of return.

Table IV.11 presents sample autocorrelations for monthly real returns on 37 Mexican stocks for the 1972-1981 period. As it was the case with nominal monthly returns, seven out the 37 first order serial correlations are statiscally different from zero. Six of the seven significant coefficients belong to the same stock that have a significant coefficient on nominal returns. Of the seven significant stocks in the overall period, two are not significant over the 1972-1976 and 1977-1981 subperiods. This can be seen in Table IV.12 and Table IV.13 respectively.

The sample autocorrelations for real returns on portfolios are given in Tables IV.14, IV.15 and IV.16. Three out of the five portfolios are significant in the 1972-1981 period, but this significance is not consistent over time.

The results of these tests on monthly real returns on individual stocks and portfolios seem to indicate weak-form inefficciency.

B. ESTIMATING STOCK AND PORTFOLIO RISK

The previous serial correlation tests do not include risk in the analysis and no one needs to be convinced of the necessity of including risk in investment analysis. The construction of a general equilibrium model will allow us to determine the relevant measure of risk for any asset and the relationship between expected return and risk for any asset when markets are in equilibrium. The controversy exists when defining what constitutes risk and how it should be measured. In this section, I perform some tests of the general equilibrium models that have been presented in the literature. In doing so, I discuss many of the problems encountered in designing these tests.

B.1. THE MARKET MODEL

This is the simplest model and it asserts that return from time (t-1) to t on asset i, Rit, is a linear function of the return on a "market portfolio", Rmt, and independent factors unique to asset i, Eit. Symbolically, this relationship takes the form

$$\tilde{Rit} = C + B \; \tilde{Rmt} + \tilde{Eit} \qquad (4.2)$$

where the tilde indicates a random variable, C is a parameter whose value is such that the expected value of Eit is zero, and B is the beta coefficient that can be interpreted as a measure of risk appropiate to asset i. The assumption that Eit is independent and unique to asset i implies that Cov (Eit,Rmt) is zero and that Cov (Eit,Ejt) $i \neq j$, are zero. This last conclusion is equivalent to assuming the absence of industry effects.

The empirical validity of the market model as it applies to stocks listed on several exchanges has been examined extensively in the literature. [See Pogue and Solnik (1974) and Sharpe (1962)]. There is a lack of corresponding studies for Mexican securities due primarily to the absence of generally available machine readable data bases. The purpose of this section is to present the results of some initial tests of the market model for a broad section of Mexican stocks.

Table IV.17 shows the results of running O.L.S. on equation (4.2) for 37 Mexican stocks. The intercept is not statistically different from zero in the mayority of cases. The range of betas goes from 0.348 to 1.416 and all of them have a coefficient that is statistically significant. The average explanatory power of the regression (adjusted R2) is approximately 20%.

In Table IV.18 it is important to note that going from individual securities to portfolios the range of betas is much lower (0.239 Vs. 1.068) and the average explanatory power much higher (54% Vs. 20%).

To establish the accuracy of the estimates, I proceeded to check the assumptions of the classical linear regression model. Specifically I performed the Durbin-Watson test for serial correlation over the 37 regressions and found that in thirteen of them the null hypothesis that the serial correlation coefficient is equal to zero was rejected in favor of the alternative hypothesis that negative serial correlation is present. This was the expected outcome from the analysis of the serial correlation tests of individual stocks. The same results were found in four out of the five portfolio regressions.

To test for heteroscedasticity, I used the absolute value of the residuals, /Ei/, to estimate

$$/Ei/ = a + b \; Rmi + Wi \qquad (4.3)$$

This test was proposed by Glejser (1969) and it is necessary to check the significance of both the intercept and the slope. Two possiblities may arise. First, if the estimated intercept does not differ significantly from zero whereas the estimated slope does, heterscedasticity is present and the original regression has to be deflated by Rmi. Second, if both the estimated intercept and the slope are significantly different from zero, heteroscedasticity is present and the original equation has to be deflated by (a+b Rmi). Finally, in all other cases, the hypothesis of homoscedasticity is accepted.

Tables IV.19 and IV.20 show that the second case is present in nine out the 37 shares and in one out of the five portfolios.

The results of negative serial correlation and heteroscedasticity are consistent with those found on returns of individual shares in Chapter III. This comes as no surprise due to the fact that both the dependent variable and the error term have the same variance-covariance structure on the classical regression model. That is $E \sim (0, T2In)$ and $Y \sim (XB, T2In)$.

In summary: a) negative serial correlation was found in ten shares and three portfolios. You can see corrections on Tables IV.21 and IV.22 using the Hildreth-Lu technique. b) heteroscedasticity was found in six shares and corrections are presented in Table IV.23. c) negative serial correlation and heteroscedasticity were found in three shares and one portfolio. Table IV.24 adjusts for heteroscedasticity first and then for serial correlation. Table IV.25 adjusts for serial correlation first and then for heteroscedasticity.

B.2. THE CAPITAL ASSET PRICING MODEL (C.A.P.M.)

In the C.A.P.M. developed and elaborated by Sharpe (1964), Litner (1965), Mossin (1960), Fama (1971), and others, the equilibrium expected rate of return of a security is related to its systematic risk (the beta coefficient) as follows:

$$E(Ri) = Rf + Bim [E(Rm) - Rf] \qquad (4.4)$$
where :

$E(Ri)$ = expected return on security i
Rf = risk-free rate
$E(Rm)$ = expected return on a market portfolio
Bim = sensitivity of security i's return to the return on the market

The difficulty one encounters in attempting to test this model is that such ex-ante expectations are not measurable directly. This can be done by assuming that the rate of return on any asset is a fair game. In this way, when the C.A.P.M. is empirically tested, it is usually writen in the following form:

$$Ri = Rf + Bim \, (Rm - Rf) + Ei \qquad (4.5)$$

$$Ri - Rf = C + Bim \, (Rm - Rf) + Ei \qquad (4.6)$$

Equation (4.5) is equal to equation (4.6) except that an intercept has been added. If equation (4.6) is used to test the validity of the C.A.P.M., one would expect to find among other things that the intercept should be statistically equal to zero.

O.L.S. was performed on shares and portfolios to estimate betas and to check if the intercept was statistically different from zero[24]. Tables IV.26 and IV.27 show that there are some intercepts statistically different from zero for individual securities but none when portfolios are formed. The range of betas runs from 0.534 to 1.352 for individual stocks and goes from 0.850 to 0.993 for portfolios. The average beta is a little less than one due to the fact that some of the stocks used to form portfolios are not part of the index used a proxy for the market. All of them have a beta coefficient that is statistically different from zero. The average explanatory power of the regression on individual securities is approximately 33% and 69% for portfolios. This compares favorably with the adjusted R2 obtanied from the Market Model.

The same kind of tests and corrections used in the Market Model were applied to the C.A.P.M. to obtain the best possible estimates. Tables IV.26 and IV.27 show the tests for serial correlation and Tables IV.28 and IV.29 present the test for heteroscedasticity.

All these tables present similar results as those obtanied in the Market Model. That is, the presence of negative serial correlation and heteroscedasticity. Corrections for serial correlation are in Tables IV.30 and IV.31. Corrections for heteroscedasticity are contanied in Table IV.32. Finally, adjustments for serial correlation and heteroscedasticity are presented in Tables IV.33 and IV.34.

---

[24] This is only the first step used in the mayor empirical tests of the C.A.P.M. like those of Blume and Friend (1970, 1973), Black, Jensen and Scholes (1973). Subsequent steps are performed in order to avoid part of the measurement errors in estimating betas of individual stocks.

C. RISK MEASUREMENT WHEN SHARES ARE
SUBJECT TO INFREQUENT TRADING

Because reported closing prices typically represent trades prior to the actual close of the trading day, measured return very often deviate from true returns. This anomaly in the way the data is collected was pointed out by Fisher (1966) who found that an index constructed from such data suffers from positive serial correlation and its estimated variance is biased downward. This is known as the "Fisher effect" and introduces into the Market Model or any other model used to estimate beta the econometric problem of errors-in variable. With errors-in variables in the Market Model, O.L.S. estimators are biased and inconsistent. The shorter the interval used to estimate returns, the more severe this problem becomes.

In particular, many shares listed in the Mexican stock exchange are traded infrequently. There are a few shares whose prices are determined and recorded every day. This can be proved by looking at Table IV.35. The price of the stock was observed every Wednesday to check whether or not it was traded on that particular day. The period covered was 1972-1981, resulting in 521 trading days. The results of Table IV.35 can be summarized as follows:

		%
Shares with trading days between 400 and 500	7	20.58
Shares with trading days between 300 and 400	13	38.24
Shares with trading days between 200 and 300	8	23.53
Shares with trading days between 100 and 200	6	17.65
	34	100.00

C.1. SCHOLES AND WILLIAMS BETA

Scholes and Williams (1977) suggested an approach for estimating the risk of infrequently traded shares. They showed that for securities not missing an observation, the following gives a consistent estimate of beta:

$$Bi = \frac{Bi\text{-}1 + Bi0 + Bi\text{+}1}{1 + 2p1} \qquad (4.7)$$

where :

Bi-1 is the parameter estimate obtanied from the simple regression of Rit against Rmt-1

Bi0 is obtanied from synchronous simple regression

Bi+1 is obtanied from the simple regression of Rit against Rmt+1

p1 is the first order serial correlation for the market index

In essence, the sum of betas estimated by regressing the return on the stock against the return on the market from previous, current and subsequent periods is divided by one plus twice the estimated autocorrelation coefficient for the market index.

The Scholes and Williams estimator (equation 4.7) was calculated for Mexican stocks and portfolios using both weekly and monthly returns. The results are presented in Tables IV.40 and IV.41. The discussion of the results is presented in section IV.4 in which I compare all the betas obtanied in this chapter.

C.2. DIMSON'S CORRECTED BETA

Dimson (1979) mentioned that the Scholes-Williams method fails to make use of share prices which are not preceeded or followed by a trade in an inmediately adjacent time period. He suggested the aggregate coefficient method. To apply it, one just needs to run a multiple regression of security return against lagged, matching and leading market returns. Then, a consistent estimate of beta can be obtanied by aggregating the slope coefficients from this regression. Formally, run O.L.S. on :

$$Rt = C + \sum_{k=-n}^{n} Bk\ Rmt+k + Ut \qquad (4.8)$$

and get

$$\hat{B} = \sum_{k=-n}^{n} Bk \qquad (4.9)$$

The appropiate selection of the parameter n represents a conflict between model and statistical accuracy. As n increases, the model becomes more realistic and less biased, but the statistical efficiency of the estimator declines. Fowler and Rorke (1983) demostrated that Dimson's estimator is not specified correctly. They developed a variant of Dimson's procedure that yields results which are similar to Scholes and Williams and therefore consistent. The estimator is given by :

$$b1 = \frac{1 + p1 + p2}{1 + 2p1 + 2p2} B1 + \frac{1 + 2p1 + p2}{1 + 2p1 + 2p2} B2 + B3 + \quad ---$$

$$--- \quad \frac{1 + p1 + p2}{1 + 2p1 + 2p2} B4 \quad \frac{1 + p1 + p2}{1 + 2p1 + 2p2} B5 \qquad (4.10)$$

Equation (4.10) is the Dimson's corrected beta, where
  p1 is the first order serial correlation coefficient for the
  market index.

p2 is the second order serial correlation for the market
index.

"Even with this modification Dimson's procedure may still be more economical than Scholes and Williams. In the example with two leads and two lags, the former only requires one multiple regression per security and two for the index. The issue then is whether one multiple regression is more expensive than several single regressions"[25]. The results of running O.L.S. on equation (4.8) with n=2 for monthly returns on securities and portfolios, as well as Dimson's corrected betas (equation 4.10), are presented in Tables IV.36 and IV.37. The corresponding results for weekly returns on securities and portfolios are given in Tables IV.38 and IV.39. It is important to note that the coefficient on the matching market return is always significant and that the coefficient in the one-period lead is also statistically significant different from zero in many cases.

---

[25] D. J. Fowler and C. H. Rorke. "Risk Measurement When Shares are Subject to Infrequent Trading." Journal of Financial Economics, (August 1983): 283.

D. A COMPARISON OF BETAS

Scholes and Williams (1977), Dimson (1979) and Fowler and Rorke (1983) present analytical as well as empirical evidence that betas of securities that trade less (more) frequently than the index used in their estimation are downward (upward) biased. This problem appears particularly severe the shorter the differencing interval. This section investigates this sort of bias within the Mexican stock market by comparing the betas estimated in section IV.C.1 and IV.C.2.

The market index published by the exchange until 1980 was based on a fixed sample of 29 stocks. The index weigthed stocks considering ony their prices and it did not adjust for subscriptions. The increased number of stocks added to the exchange in the last years of the 70's made of the index not a very good proxy of the movements of the exchange at that time. The new index overcomes all these disadvantages.

Let me first use the betas estimated using weekly returns in which the bias is suppose to be more critical. Table IV.40 presents the betas for securities and portfolios calculated using the Market Model, the C.A.P.M., the Scholes-Willimas model and the Dimson's corrected procedure. This table should be analyzed together with Table IV.35 that shows the trading frequencies of each stock.

Take the six stocks that have less than 200 trading days : ACCO, ECAT, GESA, INDE, LAMO, LORE. The Market Model or the C.A.P.M. beta is increased in all of them when estimation procedures that take into consideration trading frequency are used. In fact, beta is increased by nearly 90% in most cases.

Look now at the seven stocks that trade very frequently (those with over 400 trading days) : BANA, CARB, CELA, FUND, KIMB, LIVE, PENO. The results are mixed here. As expected KIMB and LIVE have consistently lower betas when an adjustment is made for trading frequency. FUND has a lower beta when S-W(+-2) is used and higher beta when S-W(+-1) is utilized. However, the others have S-W betas higher than Market Model or C.A.P.M. betas in approximately 15% on average.

A possible explanation for this asymmetry is that AVIA and APA, the most heavily weighted stocks in the old market index, are moderate trading stocks with 393 and 321 transaction days respectively. This is why the beta of AVIA is virtually the same no matter what method is used to estimate betas.

The results are not that convincing when betas are estimated using monthly returns (see Table IV.41). However, the differences in betas does not appear to be as high as they are when weekly returns are used.

To conclude this section, let me emphasize again the necessity of using methods that take into consideration the trading frequency to estimate betas. This requirement becomes more important the shorter the interval used to estimate returns. This is very important within the Mexican stock market in which many assets are not very active.

E. STABILITY OF BETAS OVER TIME

The previous models do not necessarily require that the beta coefficient be stable over time. However, it is important to examine the stationarity of beta for investment analysis and forecasting purposes.

Baesel (1974) indicated that the stability of beta increases substantially as the length of the estimation interval increases. To make sure the stability or non-stability of beta is captured the weekly data will be used in this section.

The stationarity of beta can be checked using the Chow test that examines for the equality between sets of coefficients in two linear regressions[26]. O.L.S. was run on equation (4.8) with n=2 over the entire period as well as two five-year subperiods. Then, the following test statistic given by the F ratio was calculated :

$$F_{(k,\ n1+n2-2k)} = \frac{ESSr - ESSur\ /\ k}{ESSur\ /\ (n1+n2-2k)} \quad (4.11)$$

where

k	=	number of parameters
n1	=	number of observations in the first subperiod
n2	=	number of observations in the second subperiod
ESSr	=	restricted residual sum of squares. That is, the sum of squared residuals in a regression over n1+n2
ESSur	=	ESS1 + ESS2 = unrestricted residual sum of squares

---

[26] R. S. Pindyck and D. L. Rubinfeld. Econometric Models and Economic Forecasts, Second Edition, McGraw-Hill, 1981., p. 123-4.

$$ESS1 = \text{residual sum of squares in a regression over } n1$$
$$ESS2 = \text{residual sum of squares in a regression over } n2$$

If the F statistic is larger than the critical value of the F distribution with k and n1+n2 degrees of freedom, the null hypothesis stating the equality of the coefficients in the subperiods can be rejected. Tables IV.42 and IV.43 show the Chow statistic on the 34 securities and the five portfolios respectively. The critical value of F is also given.

It is apparent from the tables that most securities would be classified as having non-stationarity coefficients and all the portfolios would be classified as having stationarity coefficients.

In the case of individual securities the null hypothesis is rejected. It is possible that the beta coefficients are equal and it is the intercept the one that changed. To explore this possibility O.L.S. is run on:

$$Ri = C + B1\ Rm(-2) + B2\ Rm(-1) + B3\ Rm+$$
$$B4\ Rm(1) + B5\ Rm(2) + B6\ D + Ei \qquad (4.12)$$

where D is a dummy variable that takes the value of one in the 1972-1976 subperiod and a value of zero in the 1977-1981 subperiod. Table IV.44 shows the coefficient of D as well as its corresponding t-statistic. Performing a t-test on the null hypothesis that B6=0, one can conclude that the intercept has not changed in the two subperiods. Then, the beta coefficients are the ones that changed.

These results are consistent with those of Blume (1971, 1975) who found that the beta coefficients were highly stable for portfolios containing a large number of securities but unstable for individual securities. It is reasonable to suppose that individual betas change over time in response to certain changes in the structure of corporations. This is one of the reasons that the theory of capital markets assumes people hold well-diversified portfolios. In addition, these results support the idea of using portfolios rather than individual securities for forecasting purposes because the probability of predicting an average (the beta of a portfolio) is higher than the probability of predicting the components of the average (the beta of individual securities) providing that the errors in the prediction of the components are independent of each other.

F. SERIAL CORRELATION TESTS ON EXCESS RETURNS
[R - E(R)]

Having found a way to determine the relationship between expected return and risk for any asset or group of assets, the random walk model can now be tested on excess returns. Excess return is defined here as the difference between actual return and what is expected under the C.A.P.M.. That is :

$$\text{Excess return} = Ri - E(Ri)$$
$$\text{Excess return} = Ri - [Rf + Bi(Rm-Rf)]$$
$$\text{Excess return} = Ri - [Rf + Bi(Rm) - Bi(Rf)]$$
$$\text{Excess return} = Ri - Rf - Bi(Rm) + Bi(Rf)$$
$$\text{Excess return} = Ri - Bi(Rm) - Rf(1-Bi) \qquad (4.13)$$

Equation (4.13) was calculated for weekly and monthly returns that have observations over the 1972-1981 period, and serial correlations tests were perform on both individual stocks and portfolios. However, the results of section IV.E demostrate that more emphasis should be given to portfolios when weekly returns are interpreted.

It was stated in section IV.D that the shorter the interval to calculate returns, the greater the necessity to adjust for trading frequency in estimating betas. This is why the Scholes-Williams Beta (Rm +-1) of Table IV.40 was used to estimate equation (4.13) for weekly excess returns. Table IV.45 shows the sample autocorrelations for weekly excess returns on 34 individual stocks over the 1972-1981 period. At lag one, 19 out of 34 coefficients are statistically different from zero and all of them having a negative sign. Therefore, the results found on serial correlations tests on weekly returns are more pronounced on serial correlations tests on excess weekly returns. To investigate the stationarity over time of the negative serial correlation, the 1972-1981 period was subdivided into two five-year subperiods. Table IV.46 shows the sample autocorrelations for the 1972-1976 subperiod and Table IV.47 presents the sample autocorrelations for the 1977-1981 subperiods. Of the 19 negative significant coefficients in the 1972-1981 period, 13 reappeared negative and significant in the first subperiod, and 16 manifested negative and significant in the second subperiod. Therefore, one can conclude that the negative serial correlation on excess returns for individual securities was quite consistent over the time under consideration.

The sample autocorrelations for weekly excess return on portfolios are presented in Tables IV.48, IV.49, and IV.50. Note that the "Fisher effect" found for portfolio returns on section IV.A.1, vanishes for portfolio excess returns. That is, significant negative serial correlation is obtained at lag one in four out of the five excess returns on portfolios for the 1972-1981 period. However, only one of them is consistent in the two subperiods.

The C.A.P.M. betas of Table IV.41 were used to calculate equation (4.13) for monthly excess returns. Remember that some of these betas were corrected for heteroscedasticity and/or serial correlation, and that the difference between the C.A.P.M. betas and those betas from models that take into consideration thin trading was not as pronounced as the ones obtained using weekly returns. Table IV.51 presents the sample autocorrelations for monthly excess returns on 37 stocks over the 1972-1981 period. At lag one, 15 out the 37 coefficients are statistically different from zero, and all of them have a negative sign. Tables IV.52 and IV.53 show that seven and eight of the 15 significant coefficients reappeared with the same condition in the first and second subperiods, respectively.

The sample autocorrelations for monthly excess return on portfolios are shown on Tables IV.54, IV.55, and IV.56. The results obtained for weekly excess returns on portfolios are duplicated for monthly excess returns on portfolios. Negative and significant serial correlation is present in four of the five portfolios, but only one of them is consistent in the two subperiods.

The overall results on both weekly and monthly excess returns on individual stocks as well as portfolios indicate that the Mexican stock market was weak-form innefficient in the period of time analyzed. Hoewever, this statistical significance may not be of economical importance once transactions cost are taken into consideration. This possiblity as well as some non-linear relationships are explored in the next section.

G. FILTER RULES

As indicated earlier, there may be a non-linear relationship between successive returns or price changes. For instance Rt might be related to Rt-1 in a quadratic way. One way to test for the existence of these complex combinations is to formulate a strategy appropiate for a particular pattern of returns and see what would have happened if one had actually traded under this strategy. The strategy is called in finance a "filter rule" and it shows investors when they should buy and sell a security. Filter rules are timing models. That is, they are variable-time models that seek to reveal patterns of return behavior which fixed-time models will not detect. Filter rules are analyzed by comparing them to a buy and hold strategy.

There is an infinite number of possible filter rules that can be applied, but all of them as well as all the methods of technical analysis rest on the assumption that the market repeats itself in patterns and past information is useful for prediction. Therefore, one can test specific filter rules to see if they work. Alexander (1961,1964) proposed and tested the following x percent filter: If the price of the security moves up at least x percent, buy and hold the security until its price moves down at least x percent from a subsequent high, at which time simultaneously sell and go short. The short position is maintained until the price rises at least x percent above a subsequent low, at which time one covers the short position and buys. Moves less than x percent in either direction are ignored.

Alexander (1961) tested filters from 5 to 50 percent using daily data on price indexes from 1897 to 1959. His results showed that in general filters yielded profits significantly greater than those of buy and hold. Alexander (1964) reworked his earlier results to take into account a computation bias. The bias was caused by the fact that the purchase price is generally higher than the low plus x percent, while the sale price is generally below the high minus x percent. The reworked results showed that the profitability of the filters was drastically reduced. Fama and Blume (1966) argued that Alexander's results are very difficult to interpret because it is impossible to adjust the price indexes for the effects of dividends. They compared the profitability of various filters to buy and hold policy for daily data on the individual stocks of the Dow-Jones Industrial Average. They found that most of the small filters (0.5, 1.0 and 1.5%) gave returns greater than a buy and hold strategy. They concluded, however, that once transaction costs are taken into account, the profits are eliminated.

The above filter rules are not appropiate for testing the efficiency of the Mexican stock market because short selling was not legal practice in this arena. Due to this fact, a modified version is neccesary to see if the random walk model can be refuted with particular variable-time models. Sweeney (1986), not only provides a risk adjusted rule which is very appropiate for the Mexican stock market, but also develops an statistic which compares the filter's return with a measure of its equilibrium value. Sweeney's rule has funds as either equities or risk-free assets. More specifically the rule begins the investor in the stock. If the stock's price falls z percent below its past local high, the investor sells the stock at the closing price and invests the money in the risk free rate. Then, the investor follows the stock until its price rises y percent above its past local low, at which time funds are taken from the risk free asset to buy the stock at the closing price. Using the 1970-1982 period, Sweeney reexamined the individual stocks that seem to offer potential profits in the Fama and Blume study for the .5 of one percent rule. He performed a test with statistical confidence bounds that demostrates that each security gives highly significant profits for any investor who can obtain transaction costs of .05 of one percent. Furthermore, for an equally weighted portfolio, the filter earns significant profits even when transaction costs are .15 of one percent.

The tests used by Sweeney (1986) are compatible with any equilibrium model. He defined excess returns using the observational "market model" as follows :

$$ri = Ri - Rf = Bi \ (Rm - Rf) + ei \qquad (4.14)$$

Note that this definition of excess retuns [Ri - Rf] is different from the one used in the previous section [Ri - E(Ri)]. The statistic used by Sweeney to judge filter rule profits is:

$$X = R(F) - R \ (BH) + f \ R \ (BH)$$

$$X = R \ (F) - (1 - f) \ R \ (BH) \qquad (4.15)$$

where:

    X   is the statistic developed by Sweeney to judge filter rule profits.

    R (F)   is the mean excess return on the filter which is a weighted average of the mean excess returns on days in and out of the stock.

    R (BH) is the mean excess return on a buy and hold strategy.

$$f = \frac{\text{number of days the investor is "out" of the stock (nout)}}{\text{nout + number of days the investor is "in" the stock (nin)}}$$

Sweeney proved that the expected value and standard error of X are :

$$E(X) = 0$$

$$T_X = T_r [f(1-f)]^{1/2} / N^{1/2} \quad \text{where } T_r \text{ is the st. dev. of ri.}$$

The filter rules used by Alexander and Sweeney would work if price changes or returns are positively correlated. It only makes sense to buy a stock if its price has moved up x percent, if it is likely to move up afterwards. However, the results on the Mexican stock returns displayed a preponderance of negative serial correlation. Therefore, it is appropiate to use Sweeney's filter in a reverse form. That is, it is likely that a reverse filter would work when returns are negatively correlated. The reverse filter would start the investor in the stock. Then, if the stock's price rises z percent above its past local low the investor sells the stock at the closing price and invests the money in the risk free asset. The investor follows the stock until its price drops y percent below its past local high, at which time funds are taken from the risk free rate to buy the stock at the closing price.

Both normal and reverse filters ranging from 0.5 percent to 50 percent were applied to weekly returns on 34 individual stocks and to an equally-weighted portfolio over the 1972-1981 period. The empirical work in which filters turned out to be significant is presented in detail and the results showing that filter rules did not work are giving in a summary version.

Table IV.57 presents the results of applying a 1/2 of one percent filter to individual stocks. Column (1) shows the X statistic developed by Sweeney. Its dimension is percent per week and it does not adjust for transactions costs. The X statistic is positive in 22 out the 34 stocks, meaning that RF > (1-f) RBH. Column (2) shows the standard error of X. Column (3) presents the number of transactions within the 521 business weeks over the 1972-1981 period. For example, the average number of transactions per week for ACCO is 0.22265 (116 /521). Column (4) lists the X for stocks adjusting for commissions of 0.35 of one percent. For instance, the unadjusted X value of 0.3203 for ACCO must be reduced 0.0779 (0.35x0.22265) to 0.2424. Once commissions are considered, the number of positive X's is reduced from 22 to 15. Column (5) shows the significance level of the adjusted X by dividing (4) by (2). Of the 15 positive X's, only one reached significance at the 95% confidence level.

The 0.35 of one percent transaction cost is only half the average commission for the period considered and it was only applicable to mutual funds, pension funds and brokers. The average investor would have paid at least 0.7 of one percent. The effects of four different transactions costs on the performance of an equally weighted portfolio using a 1/2 of one percent filter is presented in Table IV.58. The first column shows the X statistic for the portfolio which is simply the average X for individual stocks. The second column is the result of dividing the portfolio X mean by the standard error on Xp. In calculating the variance of Xp, it is assumed that the X's for individual securities are uncorrelated. The third column relaxes this assumption and calculates the t-statistic on Xp adjusting the variance of the portfolio with the sample covariance. The results indicate that when transaction costs are ignored, a 1/2 of one percent filter is statistically significant on an equally weighted portfolio. However, once the minimum commissions are incorporated, this significance disappears.

Tables IV.59 and IV.60 present tests for individual stocks as well as for an equally weighted portfolio using a one percent filter rule. The results are very similiar to the previous ones. Only three of the 34 stocks have a positive and significant t-statistic after transaction costs of 0.35 of one percent are considered, and the significance of an equally weighted portfolio vanishes after the inclusion of mimimum commissions.

A summary of 15 differents filter rules ranging from 0.005 to 0.500 showing the effects of transaction costs of 0.35 of one percent on both individual stocks and an equally weighted portfolio is presented in Table IV.61. First, notice that the t-statistic on Xp before commissions is only significant for the 1/2 of one percent filter rule and for the one percent filter. Second, the t-statistic on Xp after transactions costs never reaches significance. Third, the number of profitable securities whose t-statistic on X is positive and significant after adjusting for transactions costs is never bigger than three.

Let's now proceed to analyze the results of applying reverse filter rules. Table IV.62 shows a summary of 15 different reverse filter rules ranging from 0.005 to 0.500 including the effect of a 0.35% commission on individual stocks and an equally weighted portfolio. The t-statistic on Xp before transactions costs is only significant for the 25 percent reverse filter. However, this significance disappeared once minimium commissions are included. The number of profitable securities whose t-statistic on X is positive and significant after adjusting for transactions costs is never greater than four. Tables IV.63 and IV.64 present the details of the 25 percent reverse filter.

The overall results indicate that there are only a very few cases in which both normal and reverse filter rules on individual stocks beat a buy-

and-hold strategy after minimum transactions costs are considered. For an equally weighted portfolio, significance before commissions is achieved twice for normal filters and once for reverse filters. However, all the significant profits are eliminated with the inclusion of mimimun transactions costs. The results of these tests indicate that the negative serial correlation found on both returns and excess returns although statistically significant may not be of economic importance; or it may also be the case that the weekly data is not able to detect the trends of the filters, and it so, the negative serial correlation may still be of economic significance.

TABLE IV.1

SAMPLE AUTOCORRELATIONS FOR WEEKLY RETURNS ON 91 MEXICAN
STOCKS FOR LAGS L=1,2,3,......8
1972-1981

****

STOCK	1	2	3	4	5	6	7	8	T
ACCI	-.152	.228	-.095	.053	-.013	.067	.052	-.025	59
ACCO	-.020	.002	.029	.033	-.102*	.009	.018	-.001	521
ACEY	-.083	.072	-.049	.034	-.002	.087	-.037	.041	521
ALFA	-.081	.093	.143	.028	.234*	-.010	.037	.307*	178
ALTR	-.129	-.076	.045	-.031	.047	-.041	.064	.016	157
ALUM	-.130*	-.073	-.008	.047	-.062	-.050	.017	.005	521
APAS	-.076	.141*	-.042	.011	-.030	-.047	.033	-.029	521
AURR	-.372*	.055	.037	-.002	-.013	.071	-.021	.043	266
AUTL	.009	-.038	-.007	.017	-.026	.001	.097	-.022	347
AVIA	-.140*	-.083	.167*	-.044	.008	.037	.012	.042	521
BACA	-.008	.034	-.125*	.037	-.016	.000	.053	.028	521
BANA	-.205*	-.018	-.116*	.114*	.019	-.015	.004	.006	521
BANC	-.103	-.005	.045	.040	-.004	.194*	.042	-.034	209
BCH	-.131*	-.024	.049	.005	-.071	.074	-.004	.050	520
BDCO	.164*	-.050	.176*	.128*	-.095	-.052	.162*	-.019	312
BIMB	-.250*	-.053	.065	.095	-.024	-.087	.027	.139	98
BIME	.132*	.002	-.045	-.025	-.004	.015	-.030	-.038	521
CAME	-.052	.133	-.022	-.011	.076	.003	.135	.073	153
CAMP	-.016	-.064	-.062	.033	.024	-.040	.051	.014	521
CANA	-.049	.052	-.021	-.036	.082	.075	.007	-.007	474
CANN	-.007	.035	.036	-.004	.009	-.003	-.152*	.031	521

****

TABLE IV. 1 (CONTINUED)

STOCK	1	2	3	4	5	6	7	8	T
CARB	-.170*	-.051	-.017	-.027	.009	.018	-.009	.100*	521
CECH	-.173*	.048	.036	-.018	.025	.051	-.049	.069	416
CELA	-.270*	-.108*	.160*	-.048	.010	-.049	.040	.055	521
CEME	-.041	-.003	-.011	.022	.153*	-.064	.006	-.021	203
CENM	.093*	-.017	.077	-.009	-.036	.018	-.008	-.028	521
CERM	-.014	.076	.053	-.108*	.023	-.089	-.018	.057	521
CIGA	-.114	.020	.070	.012	.051	.008	.017	-.029	274
CODU	.067	.052	.000	.035	.036	.002	.017	.015	261
COME	-.033	.006	.050	.082	.027	.084	-.089	.082	209
COMZ	-.021	.007	.019	.032	.038	-.008	-.005	.073	209
CONF	-.226*	.166*	-.096	.054	-.074	.027	.067	-.005	138
CONT	.124	.012	-.081	.014	.041	.042	-.028	.039	135
CREM	-.212*	-.072	-.054	-.024	.127	.009	-.080	-.002	144
CRIS	.014	.107*	.032	.052	-.072	.009	.063	.045	521
DIAN	.013	.033	-.022	.010	-.024	.048	.036	.079	519
DOMI	-.027	-.084	-.029	-.078	-.096	.058	.111	.003	179
EATO	-.020	.013	-.013	.078	.023	-.036	-.014	.068	521
ECAT	.084	-.005	-.022	.001	-.001	.013	.064	.065	521
EPEN	-.016	-.100	.004	.045	-.015	.024	-.032	-.051	173
ERIC	-.028	.069	-.046	-.030	.040	.008	.049	.152*	270
FRIS	.024	.032	-.037	.094*	.098*	.036	-.044	-.057	521
FUND	-.026	-.119*	.029	.017	-.037	.105*	-.063	-.048	521
GESA	.067	.009	.043	.107*	.047	.003	.047	.032	521
GISS	.107	-.081	-.033	.022	.080	.043	-.053	-.025	261

TABLE IV. 1 (CONTINUED)

STOCK	1	2	3	4	5	6	7	8	T
GPOM	-.095	-.092	-.004	-.025	.051	-.018	-.033	.059	230
GPOM	.101	.015	-.062	-.035	.032	.111	-.232*	.010	105
HOOK	.066	.082	.144*	.041	.030	-.015	.043	-.078	249
HULC	.095	-.035	.056	-.034	.022	.017	.099	.126	187
IEM	.031	-.004	.023	-.116*	-.031	-.060	.045	.076	521
IESA	-.025	.047	.025	-.042	.066	-.185*	-.081	-.024	182
INDE	.040	-.039	-.002	-.007	.029	-.009	.034	.008	521
IRSA	-.238*	.014	-.047	.025	.012	.043	-.064	-.048	502
ITEN	.046	.056	-.035	.067	.026	-.023	-.043	.016	157
JDEE	.153*	.123	.135*	.030	.052	-.021	.022	.065	217
KELS	-.070	-.022	.058	-.070	-.032	-.003	-.003	-.042	162
KIMB	-.248*	-.065	-.003	.015	-.001	.032	.002	-.006	521
LAMO	.062	-.013	.018	.001	-.004	.018	.093	.073	521
LIVE	-.226*	-.009	-.020	.068	-.028	.032	-.028	-.070	521
LORE	-.005	-.015	-.048	-.003	-.045	-.066	.030	-.002	521
LUIS	-.044	.050	-.023	.006	-.032	-.029	.002	.021	521
MARN	.097	-.165	.104	.260*	.133	-.027	-.118	.072	57
MART	.002	-.058	-.021	-.076	.014	.093	.005	.026	328
META	.169*	.150*	.070	.109	.125	.168*	.002	.068	179
MODE	-.048	.024	.033	.044	.012	-.008	.015	.051	470
NEGR	-.066	-.199*	.010	.031	.026	.021	.014	-.031	521
PALA	-.096*	.048	.131*	-.016	.084	-.058	-.030	-.035	521
PARI	-.157*	-.067	-.027	.054	.106*	-.047	-.046	-.010	469
PARR	-.269*	.147	-.014	-.155	.056	.056	.008	.179	63

TABLE IV. 1 (CONTINUED)

STOCK	1	2	3	4	5	6	7	8	T
PENO	-.068	-.064	-.039	.060	.054	-.017	-.043	.001	521
PENW	-.129	.060	.073	-.095	-.058	-.026	.023	-.077	141
PERK	-.058	-.140	-.030	.074	-.063	.013	-.074	-.020	80
PETR	-.067	-.068	.010	.027	.123*	.010	.017	-.015	344
POPO	-.084	-.046	.177*	-.137	-.055	-.048	.073	.026	151
PURN	-.070	.036	.046	-.022	.073	.054	-.001	.078	183
PURT	-.042	.005	.006	-.022	.024	.052	-.068	.008	261
REYN	-.166*	-.038	-.139*	-.140*	.038	.039	.017	-.079	209
ROBE	-.139	-.049	.002	.040	.124	.099	-.181*	.118	187
SANB	-.130*	-.028	.126*	-.109*	.018	.005	.043	.066	521
SELM	.013	.015	-.057	.052	.055	.092	.027	-.102	209
SPIC	-.127*	.083	-.046	.108*	-.023	-.038	-.010	.047	521
SUDI	-.096	-.057	.104	-.043	.028	.122*	.007	.021	282
SYR	-.094	.176	-.082	.044	-.053	-.279*	-.166	-.025	42
TAMS	-.117*	.056	-.031	.044	.017	.001	-.021	-.050	521
TEXA	-.016	.002	.061	-.019	.074	.096	-.021	.007	156
TOLM	-.060	.122*	-.039	.010	.105	.053	.051	-.027	261
TOLT	-.210*	.031	-.141*	-.008	.032	-.059	.045	-.027	308
TREM	-.037	.004	.020	.024	.032	.111*	.121*	.051	521
TUAC	-.066	-.102	.088	-.004	-.122	.029	.015	-.020	147
VIRR	-.128	.127	-.070	.024	.019	.075	.085	.022	177
VISA	-.249*	.077	.094	-.029	.040	.189*	-.019	.157*	172
VITR	-.012	.091	.000	.090	-.123	.090	-.019	.013	157

TABLE IV. 1 (CONTINUED)

* Sample autocorrelation is at least two standard errors to the left or to the right of its expected value under the hypothesis that the true autocorrelation is zero.

If the return series has been generated by a white noise, the sample autocorrelation coefficients for $L > 0$ are approximately distributed according to a normal distribution with mean zero and standard deviation $1/\text{sq.root}$ of T. Thus, if a stock has 521 observations, one can assign a standard error of .044 to the first autocorrelation coefficient. Then, if the first autocorrelation coefficient was greater than .088, one would be 95% sure that the true autocorrelation coefficient is not zero.

TABLE IV.2

SAMPLE AUTOCORRELATIONS FOR WEEKLY RETURNS ON 28 MEXICAN STOCKS FOR LAGS L=1,2,3,......8

SUBPERIOD 1

STOCK	1	2	3	4	5	6	7	8	T
ALUM	-.102	-.076	.068	-.043	-.159*	-.066	.037	-.009	260
AURR	-.238*	-.031	.202*	-.212*	.143	-.154	-.033	.163	133
AVIA	-.152*	-.126*	.117	-.034	-.083	.000	.022	-.026	260
BANA	-.038	.028	.061	.038	.034	.020	-.046	-.094	260
BCH	-.112	-.089	-.018	.071	-.005	.020	.042	-.006	260
BDCO	-.059	-.057	-.007	.076	-.063	-.099	.067	-.239*	156
BIMB	.130	-.058	.180	.163	.140	-.090	.020	.334*	50
BIME	.044	.046	-.080	-.006	-.041	.069	.064	-.109	260
CARB	-.131*	-.038	.002	-.021	.048	-.105	.050	.115	260
CECH	-.149*	-.024	-.030	.025	.014	-.024	-.023	-.009	208
CELA	-.180*	-.035	-.108	.017	.076	-.071	-.056	.090	260
CENM	.054	-.108	.046	-.181*	-.074	.104	-.039	-.004	260
CONF	-.333*	.281*	-.224	.182	-.210	.204	-.010	.122	69
CREM	-.168	-.162	-.034	-.188	.218	.096	-.199	.034	72
IRSA	-.265*	.072	-.100	.064	.037	.002	-.041	-.028	251
JDEE	.218*	.178	-.002	.012	-.007	-.174	.018	.065	109
KIMB	-.147*	-.043	-.024	.110	-.056	.011	-.098	-.009	260
LIVE	-.308*	.024	-.083	.085	-.055	.061	-.022	-.101	260
META	.229*	.135	.095	.081	.133	.212	-.016	.110	90
PALA	-.151*	-.037	.037	-.008	-.061	.018	.021	-.056	260
PARI	-.150*	-.064	-.055	-.010	.032	-.034	.036	.013	234

TABLE IV.2 (CONTINUED)

****

STOCK	1	2	3	4	5	6	7	8	T
PARR	-.222	-.043	.031	-.244	.055	.029	-.285	.301	32
REYN	.363*	-.068	-.265*	-.206	.032	.054	-.026	-.065	104
SANB	-.071	-.153*	.175*	-.030	-.064	.051	.058	-.063	260
SPIC	-.084	-.020	-.012	.018	.016	-.120	-.018	-.070	260
TAMS	-.212*	-.062	-.051	.108	-.042	-.007	.040	-.017	260
TOLT	-.206*	-.034	.009	.078	.099	-.174*	.150	-.006	154
VISA	-.353*	.046	.034	-.043	-.013	.204	-.045	.119	86

****

* Sample autocorrelation is at least two standard errors to the left or to the right of its expected value under the hypothesis that the true autocorrelation is zero.

If the return series has been generated by a white noise, the sample autocorrelation coefficients for L > 0 are approximately distributed according to a normal distribution with mean zero and standard deviation 1/sq.root of T. Thus, if a stock has 260 observations, one can assign a standard error of .062 to the first autocorrelation coefficient. Then, if the first autocorrelation coefficient was grater than .124, one would be 95% sure that the true autocorrelation coefficient is not zero.

TABLE IV.3

SAMPLE AUTOCORRELATIONS FOR WEEKLY RETURNS ON 28 MEXICAN STOCKS FOR LAGS L=1,2,3,......8

SUBPERIOD 2

STOCK	1	2	3	4	5	6	7	8	T
ALUM	-.140*	-.073	-.069	.096	.004	-.045	-.006	.020	261
AURR	-.393*	.059	.026	.017	-.031	.064	-.027	.014	133
AVIA	-.129*	-.045	.207*	-.055	.093	.077	-.003	.099	261
BANA	-.232*	-.026	-.146*	.124	.017	-.023	.016	-.019	261
BCH	-.139*	-.004	.087	-.036	-.102	.105	-.024	.072	260
BDCO	.170*	-.073	.178*	.116	-.124	-.072	.156	-.014	156
BIMB	-.332*	-.062	-.004	.044	-.028	-.116	.000	.119	48
BIME	.157*	-.012	-.042	-.022	.000	-.012	-.072	-.022	261
CARB	-.200*	-.062	-.033	-.037	-.018	.118	-.051	.084	261
CECH	-.188*	.094	.079	-.045	.032	.099	-.067	.119	208
CELA	-.287*	-.121	.200*	-.061	-.003	-.048	.054	.044	261
CENM	.102	.006	.085	.035	-.026	-.005	-.001	-.034	261
CONF	-.138	.053	.020	-.083	.053	-.150	.186	-.099	69
CREM	-.326*	.040	-.105	.234	-.046	-.130	.106	-.084	72
IRSA	-.220*	-.019	-.009	.010	-.002	.066	-.068	-.068	251
JDEE	.003	-.009	.297*	.001	.082	.155	-.031	.006	108
KIMB	-.278*	-.073	.002	-.013	.013	.040	.031	-.007	261
LIVE	-.190*	-.023	.006	.061	-.019	.024	-.032	-.054	261
META	-.077	.182	-.020	.189	.130	.003	.109	-.083	89
PALA	-.084	.066	.152*	-.017	.117	-.075	-.042	-.029	261
PARI	-.163*	-.070	-.008	.097	.156*	-.058	-.104	-.029	235

TABLE IV.3 (CONTINUED)

STOCK	1	2	3	4	5	6	7	8	T
PARR	-.459*	.241	-.139	-.145	.036	-.046	.069	-.013	31
REYN	-.107	-.027	-.002	-.083	.020	-.007	.042	-.131	105
SANB	-.157*	.027	.103	-.143*	.052	-.013	.036	.115	261
SPIC	-.153*	.137*	-.067	.150*	-.044	.003	-.008	.105	261
TAMS	-.098	.082	-.037	.015	.026	-.008	-.055	-.053	261
TOLT	-.212*	.054	-.198*	-.040	.006	-.015	.005	-.035	154
VISA	.103	.149	.197	.004	.135	.002	-.015	.203	86

* Sample autocorrelation is at least two standard errors to the left or to the right of its expected value under the hypothesis that the true autocorrelation is zero.
If the return series has been generated by a white noise, the sample autocorrelation coefficients for L > 0 are approximately distributed according to a normal distribution with mean zero and standard deviation 1/sq.root of T. Thus, if a stock has 133 observations, one can assign a standard error of .087 to the first autocorrelation coefficient. Then, if the first autocorrelation coefficient was grater than .174, one would be 95% sure that the true autocorrelation coefficient is not zero.

TABLE IV.4

SAMPLE AUTOCORRELATIONS ON WEEKLY
PORTFOLIO RETURNS FOR LAGS L=1,2,...8
1972-1981

****

PORT	1	2	3	4	5	6	7	8	T
Portf1	.024	.152*	.079	.019	.065	.016	.017	.065	521
Portf2	.155*	.168*	.051	.125*	.013	-.004	.003	.037	521
Portf3	.211*	.183*	.070	.055	.088*	.052	.086*	.079	521
Portf4	.068	.051	.037	.042	.039	.010	.088*	.013	521
Portf5	.059	.022	-.046	.063	.002	-.023	.009	-.043	521

****

E. W. P.	.237*	.201*	.085	.092	.079	.042	.086	.052	521
M. V. P.	.020	.104*	.037	.071	.106*	.036	.016	.053	521

****

* Significant at the 95% confidence level.

TABLE IV.5

SAMPLE AUTOCORRELATIONS FOR MONTHLY RETURNS
ON 37 MEXICAN STOCKS FOR LAGS L=1,2,..8
1972-1981

STOCK	1	2	3	4	5	6	7	8	T
ACEY	-.029	.140	.125	.186*	.025	.035	.036	-.037	120
ALUM	-.199*	-.044	.081	.011	.084	-.054	.014	-.065	120
APAS	-.073	.010	.235*	-.037	.157	-.040	.031	-.051	120
AVIA	.228*	.050	.159	.042	.049	.082	.066	-.036	120
BACA	-.006	.100	-.132	.012	-.074	.139	-.028	.154	120
BANA	.074	-.008	.049	-.073	.061	.133	-.015	.033	120
BCH	-.383*	.316*	-.118	.045	.001	.117	-.207*	.150	120
CAMP	-.032	-.123	-.069	-.073	.042	-.041	.008	-.113	120
CANN	.043	.145	.078	.065	.063	.113	.074	.112	120
CARB	-.055	.173	-.128	.057	.002	.027	-.051	.097	120
CELA	-.004	.110	.167	.035	.051	.038	.163	.053	120
CENM	-.068	-.065	.252*	-.113	.086	.171	-.020	.052	120
CERM	-.096	.090	.073	-.005	.036	.031	.147	.072	120
CRIS	.044	.253*	.055	.058	.154	.063	.146	.086	120
DIAN	-.225*	.005	-.041	-.020	-.055	.008	.017	.026	120
EATO	.097	.037	.131	.125	.156	.017	-.097	.004	120
ECAT	.040	.060	.020	-.091	-.011	-.049	-.062	-.050	120
FRIS	.271*	.119	.040	.078	.042	-.016	-.081	-.067	120
FUND	.055	-.040	.002	-.035	-.080	.089	.015	-.083	120
GESA	-.032	.163	.091	-.035	-.022	.060	-.031	.010	120
IEM	-.005	-.030	.245*	.006	-.064	-.033	.063	.109	120

TABLE IV.5 (CONTINUED)

****

STOCK	1	2	3	4	5	6	7	8	T
INDE	-.065	.047	-.005	.130	.051	-.056	-.137	.103	120
KIMB	-.184*	-.053	.011	-.031	.073	.003	.025	.063	120
LAMO	-.119	.200*	.140	.037	.083	-.054	.045	.202*	120
LIVE	.105	-.011	.261*	.026	.057	.112	-.008	.017	120
LORE	-.008	.015	.021	-.241*	-.087	-.024	.173	.159	120
LUIS	-.014	.015	-.003	-.040	-.009	.014	-.074	.095	120
MODE	.172	-.039	.080	.155	-.016	-.076	.100	.148	120
MORE	.109	.141	.115	.021	-.053	.084	-.190*	.015	120
NAFI	.250*	.229*	.049	-.024	-.063	-.283*	-.058	-.151	120
NEGR	-.051	.025	-.036	.036	-.004	-.027	-.030	.000	120
PALA	.120	.086	.051	.062	.087	-.088	-.111	-.019	120
PENO	-.077	.039	-.028	.109	.128	-.064	.018	-.050	120
SANB	.104	.063	.088	-.055	.055	.094	.016	-.082	120
SPIC	.127	-.020	.064	.025	.108	-.065	-.053	.075	120
TAMS	.082	.112	.066	.067	.154	.063	-.050	.171	120
TREM	.042	.298*	.241*	.136	.063	.047	.055	-.089	120

****

* Sample autocorrelation is at least two standard errors to the left or to the right of its expected value under the hypothesis that the true autocorrelation is zero.

If the return series has been generated by a white noise, the sample autocorrelation coefficients for $L > 0$ are approximately distributed according to a normal distribution with mean zero and standard deviation $1/\text{sq.root of } T$. Thus, if a stock has 120 observations, one can assign a standard error of .091 to the first autocorrelation coefficient. Then, if the first autocorrelation coefficient was greater than .182 one would be 95% sure that the true autocorrelation coefficient is not zero.

TABLE IV.6

SAMPLE AUTOCORRELATIONS FOR MONTHLY RETURNS
ON 37 MEXICAN STOCKS FOR LAGS L=1,2,...8
1972-1976

****

STOCK	1	2	3	4	5	6	7	8	T
ACEY	-.055	.032	.211	.061	-.050	-.019	-.092	.060	60
ALUM	-.191	-.173	.059	.086	.099	.023	.022	-.135	60
APAS	.236	.203	.244*	-.045	-.135	-.184	-.240*	-.197	60
AVIA	.118	-.043	.167	.184	.040	.074	.204	-.087	60
BACA	-.112	.046	-.230	-.131	-.027	.189	.248*	.107	60
BANA	.048	.070	.105	.005	-.011	.053	.095	.007	60
BCH	.223	-.047	.169	.135	.016	.013	-.119	-.092	60
CAMP	-.070	-.210	-.166	-.003	.150	-.077	.074	-.109	60
CANN	-.025	.095	.011	-.008	-.039	.096	-.069	.114	60
CARB	-.061	.184	-.192	.077	.069	.026	-.121	.044	60
CELA	-.149	-.105	.104	-.107	.198	-.138	-.056	.176	60
CENM	-.174	.044	.077	-.020	.160	.085	-.086	.036	60
CERM	-.060	-.084	-.135	.005	.020	.091	.035	.066	60
CRIS	-.186	.083	-.030	-.087	.038	-.118	-.055	.048	60
DIAN	-.307*	.035	-.037	-.021	-.042	-.016	-.028	-.035	60
EATO	.151	-.033	.000	.072	.135	-.128	-.180	-.031	60
ECAT	-.116	.126	-.061	.041	-.024	.025	-.052	-.025	60
FRIS	.209	-.145	.240	.218	.101	.147	-.022	.068	60
FUND	.011	-.098	-.020	.005	.171	-.149	-.012	.116	60
GESA	-.047	-.017	-.151	.045	.173	-.110	.008	.081	60
IEM	-.089	-.026	-.253	.069	.128	-.016	-.125	.143	60

TABLE IV.6 (CONTINUED)

STOCK	1	2	3	4	5	6	7	8	T
INDE	-.055	.001	.043	.061	.042	-.065	-.043	-.077	60
KIMB	-.162	-.090	-.044	-.094	.233	-.107	.020	.059	60
LAMO	-.252*	.142	.168	-.201	-.019	-.100	-.204	.160	60
LIVE	-.122	-.256*	.237	-.158	.041	.096	-.008	.051	60
LORE	-.012	-.239	-.084	.228	.032	-.098	.032	.196	60
LUIS	.045	.129	-.092	-.062	-.082	.078	-.057	.019	60
MODE	.092	-.320*	-.098	.082	-.016	-.282*	-.146	.251*	60
MORE	.353*	.185	.091	.190	.195	.005	-.016	-.054	60
NAFI	-.033	.013	.259*	-.169	-.173	.275*	-.008	-.073	60
NEGR	-.101	-.056	.000	-.143	.239*	.103	-.044	.101	60
PALA	-.123	-.124	-.100	.102	.029	.095	.001	-.024	60
PENO	-.320*	-.027	-.164	.237	-.074	-.087	.060	.039	60
SANB	-.065	.173	.280*	-.058	.144	.135	.045	.076	60
SPIC	-.073	-.022	.069	-.159	.330*	-.182	-.078	.076	60
TAMS	-.020	-.143	.035	-.094	.109	-.142	-.047	.109	60
TREM	-.011	.026	-.171	-.072	.083	-.113	-.215	-.088	60

* Sample autocorrelation is at least two standard errors to the left or to the right of its expected value under the hypothesis that the true autocorrelation is zero.

If the return series has been generated by a white noise, the sample autocorrelation coefficients for L > 0 are approximately distributed according to a normal distribution with mean zero and standard deviation 1/sq.root of T. Thus, if a stock has 60 observations, one can assign a standard error of .129 to the first autocorrelation coefficient. Then, if the first autocorrelation coefficient was greater than .258 one would be 95% sure that the true autocorrelation coefficient is not zero.

TABLE IV.7

SAMPLE AUTOCORRELATIONS FOR MONTHLY RETURNS
ON 37 MEXICAN STOCKS FOR LAGS L=1,2,..8
1977-1981

****

STOCK	1	2	3	4	5	6	7	8	T
ACEY	-.030	.179	.077	.246*	.038	.064	.097	-.092	60
ALUM	-.212	.061	.103	-.017	.045	-.211	.052	-.011	60
APAS	-.146	-.051	.195	-.094	.145	-.083	.032	-.073	60
AVIA	.367*	.158	.135	-.088	.016	.042	-.035	.027	60
BACA	-.012	.087	-.147	.012	-.126	.105	-.108	.118	60
BANA	.081	-.040	.027	-.087	.103	.152	-.063	.052	60
BCH	-.474*	.364*	-.156	.027	-.036	.122	-.192	.162	60
CAMP	.032	-.008	.077	-.139	-.136	-.008	-.102	-.109	60
CANN	.099	.188	.110	.100	.150	.040	.167	.055	60
CARB	-.042	.152	-.019	.098	-.105	.036	-.005	.116	60
CELA	.012	.149	.165	.047	.017	.056	.193	-.002	60
CENM	-.045	-.094	.291*	-.140	.066	.187	-.014	.048	60
CERM	-.111	.119	.108	-.005	.033	.013	.161	.048	60
CRIS	.057	.258*	.034	.051	.134	.080	.116	.050	60
DIAN	-.051	-.104	-.082	-.044	-.110	.058	.090	.155	60
EATO	.000	-.016	.097	.068	.132	.049	-.159	-.103	60
ECAT	.144	-.012	.071	-.137	.013	-.033	-.057	-.106	60
FRIS	.288*	.170	-.039	.046	-.020	-.132	-.072	-.058	60
FUND	.058	-.023	-.025	-.030	-.139	.085	.059	-.138	60
GESA	-.027	.224	.174	-.063	-.093	.121	-.036	-.010	60
IEM	.006	-.039	.348*	-.024	-.115	-.065	.089	.081	60

****

TABLE IV.7 (CONTINUED)

****

STOCK	1	2	3	4	5	6	7	8	T
INDE	-.073	.071	-.042	.180	.058	-.051	-.217	.182	60
KIMB	-.206	-.021	.033	.004	.009	.055	.012	.059	60
LAMO	.043	.258*	.119	.217	.128	-.037	.190	.149	60
LIVE	.211	.104	.295*	.095	.066	.184	-.001	-.019	60
LORE	-.011	.028	.023	-.272	-.096	-.018	.180	.160	60
LUIS	-.067	-.072	.053	-.044	.058	-.065	-.063	.064	60
MODE	.223	.100	.111	.184	-.002	.033	.190	.062	60
MORE	.040	.119	.104	-.050	-.136	.078	-.238*	.039	60
NAFI	.277*	.240	.039	-.022	-.061	-.336*	-.074	-.159	60
NEGR	-.044	.042	-.058	.091	-.117	-.094	-.035	-.087	60
PALA	.171	.129	.082	.054	.104	-.117	-.137	-.023	60
PENO	.107	.069	.040	.019	.302*	-.052	-.112	-.027	60
SANB	.175	.017	.013	-.048	.019	.059	.026	-.103	60
SPIC	.207	-.024	.049	.109	.004	-.037	-.028	.043	60
TAMS	.070	.156	.028	.129	.166	.013	-.074	.201	60
TREM	.038	.328*	.290*	.148	.051	.052	.069	-.109	60

****

* Sample autocorrelation is at least two standard errors to the left or to the right of its expected value under the hypothesis that the true autocorrelation is zero.

If the return series has been generated by a white noise, the sample autocorrelation coefficients for L > 0 are approximately distributed according to a normal distribution with mean zero and standard deviation 1/sq.root of T. Thus, if a stock has 60 observations, one can assign a standard error of .129 to the first autocorrelation coefficient. Then, if the first autocorrelation coefficient was greater than .258 one would be 95% sure that the true autocorrelation coefficient is not zero.

TABLE IV.8

SAMPLE AUTOCORRELATIONS ON MONTHLY PORTFOLIO
RETURNS FOR LAGS L=1,2...8
1972-1981

PORT	1	2	3	4	5	6	7	8	T
Port. 1	.278*	.210*	.134	-.006	.117	-.043	.021	.053	120
Port. 2	.155	.133	.067	-.006	.011	.052	.009	.168	120
Port. 3	.190*	.259*	.274*	.133	.075	.092	-.039	.139	120
Port. 4	.176	.008	.131	.020	-.009	.012	.003	.010	120
Port. 5	.097	-.019	.123	.039	.103	-.076	-.028	.045	120
E.W.P.	.281*	.145	.192*	.022	.087	.023	-.013	.098	120
M.V.P.	.320*	.160	.142	.050	.020	.063	-.044	.048	120
Inflation	.777*	.661*	.589*	.553*	.540*	.554*	.516*	.492*	120

* Significant at the 95% confidence level.

TABLE IV.9

SAMPLE AUTOCORRELATIONS ON MONTHLY PORTFOLIO
RETURNS FOR LAGS L=1,2,..8
1972-1976

****

PORT	1	2	3	4	5	6	7	8	T
Port. 1	-.016	-.127	.223	-.091	.165	-.078	-.274*	.212	60
Port. 2	.020	-.060	.024	.055	.247*	-.070	-.150	.120	60
Port. 3	.050	.170	.145	.006	.255*	-.029	-.073	.114	60
Port. 4	-.062	-.189	-.025	.108	.000	-.013	-.054	.015	60
Port. 5	-.049	-.297*	-.097	.041	.210	-.161	-.094	.052	60
E.W.P.	.018	-.118	.068	-.027	.242*	-.089	-.158	.105	60
M.V.P.	-.041	.062	-.173	-.003	.027	.188	-.229	.100	60
Inflation	.722*	.350*	.087	-.013	-.013	.004	.058	.124	60

****

* Significant at the 95% confidence level.

TABLE IV.10

SAMPLE AUTOCORRELATIONS ON MONTHLY PORTFOLIO
RETURNS FOR LAGS L=1,2,...8
1977-1981

****

PORT	1	2	3	4	5	6	7	8	T
Port. 1	.319*	.259*	.091	-.021	.084	-.086	.048	-.009	60
Port. 2	.178	.171	.053	-.047	-.082	.071	.046	.137	60
Port. 3	.221	.277*	.296*	.161	.005	.111	-.021	.114	60
Port. 4	.310*	.122	.206	-.029	.006	.017	.028	.015	60
Port. 5	.174	.130	.217	.041	.082	-.090	.013	-.002	60

****

E.W.P.	.354*	.220	.208	.022	.033	.023	.025	.061	60
M.V.P.	.414*	.180	.210	.067	.005	.004	-.015	.007	60

****

Inflation	.658*	.520*	.439*	.413*	.432*	.485*	.418*	.360*	60

****

* Significant at the 95% confidence level.

TABLE IV.11

SAMPLE AUTOCORRELATIONS FOR MONTHLY REAL
RETURNS ON 37 MEXICAN STOCKS FOR LAGS L=1,2,..8
1972-1981

STOCK	1	2	3	4	5	6	7	8	T
ACEY	-.017	.150	.137	.204*	.040	.044	.043	-.024	120
ALUM	-.187*	-.041	.085	.003	.092	-.045	.002	-.067	120
APAS	-.057	.017	.240*	-.027	.161	-.037	.024	-.057	120
AVIA	.241*	.068	.178	.065	.064	.093	.077	-.022	120
BACA	-.012	.106	-.129	.015	-.066	.148	-.031	.159	120
BANA	.085	.004	.075	-.039	.084	.152	-.001	.057	120
BCH	-.385*	.317*	-.111	.052	.003	.120	-.204	.151	120
CAMP	-.039	-.127	-.070	-.058	.056	-.035	.008	-.107	120
CANN	.054	.157	.083	.079	.072	.121	.072	.116	120
CARB	-.037	.181	-.106	.089	.015	.043	-.046	.107	120
CELA	.019	.125	.180	.061	.073	.061	.162	.067	120
CENM	-.040	-.045	.272*	-.102	.089	.184	-.018	.064	120
CERM	-.084	.104	.082	.013	.046	.037	.148	.085	120
CRIS	.050	.261*	.067	.075	.162	.078	.144	.093	120
DIAN	-.226*	.011	-.040	-.018	-.055	.015	.018	.030	120
EATO	.107	.044	.134	.137	.161	.025	-.101	.004	120
ECAT	.054	.065	.022	-.089	-.010	-.044	-.057	-.040	120
FRIS	.254*	.113	.046	.090	.054	.001	-.079	-.056	120
FUND	.054	-.029	.021	-.030	-.069	.092	.007	-.080	120
GESA	-.011	.172	.086	-.013	.004	.073	-.031	.020	120
IEM	-.002	-.027	.259*	.016	-.049	-.026	.067	.114	120

TABLE IV.11 (CONTINUED)

****

STOCK	1	2	3	4	5	6	7	8	T
INDE	-.063	.052	.003	.146	.070	-.058	-.124	.102	120
KIMB	-.170	-.040	.023	-.015	.082	.011	.016	.070	120
LAMO	-.086	.223*	.150	.037	.089	-.042	.046	.197	120
LIVE	.126	.000	.260*	.043	.078	.134	.008	.016	120
LORE	-.004	.021	.021	-.243*	-.087	-.023	.166	.164	120
LUIS	-.011	.026	.006	-.019	-.002	.021	-.076	.098	120
MODE	.187*	-.027	.098	.159	-.004	-.063	.097	.146	120
MORE	.116	.158	.130	.034	-.037	.096	-.184	.013	120
NAFI	.263*	.231*	.059	.006	-.044	-.254*	-.045	-.134	120
NEGR	-.036	.030	-.018	.050	.026	-.006	-.023	.001	120
PALA	.135	.099	.071	.079	.110	-.054	-.094	-.023	120
PENO	-.093	.039	-.020	.115	.133	-.067	.020	-.046	120
SANB	.104	.055	.086	-.056	.055	.095	.014	-.070	120
SPIC	.141	-.005	.070	.045	.127	-.056	-.058	.088	120
TAMS	.097	.119	.073	.075	.166	.064	-.060	.164	120
TREM	.055	.305*	.251*	.152	.073	.060	.065	-.080	120

****

* Sample autocorrelation is at least two standard errors to the left or or to the right of its expected value under the hypothesis that the true autocorrelation is zero.
If the return series has been generated by a white noise, the sample autocorrelation coefficients for L > 0 are approximately distributed according to a normal distribution with mean zero and standard deviation 1/sq.root of T. Thus, if a stock has 120 observations, one can assign a standard error of .091 to the first autocorrelation coefficient. Then, if the first autocorrelation coefficient was greater than .182 one would be 95% sure that the true autocorrelation coefficient is not zero.

TABLE IV.12

SAMPLE AUTOCORRELATIONS FOR MONTHLY REAL
RETURNS ON 37 MEXICAN STOCKS FOR LAGS L=1,2,..8
1972-1976

STOCK	1	2	3	4	5	6	7	8	T
ACEY	-.038	.047	.225	.077	-.025	-.015	-.090	.056	60
ALUM	-.152	-.161	.053	.075	.102	.022	.001	-.135	60
APAS	.309*	.247	.252	.004	-.106	-.156	-.244	-.214	60
AVIA	.135	-.020	.182	.194	.051	.080	.207	-.081	60
BACA	-.106	.069	-.191	-.107	.009	.194	.247	.128	60
BANA	.084	.090	.132	.059	.022	.050	.099	.016	60
BCH	.265*	-.010	.209	.157	.024	.043	-.064	-.053	60
CAMP	-.076	-.220	-.171	.016	.164	-.076	.070	-.108	60
CANN	-.008	.106	.018	.005	-.032	.096	-.070	.112	60
CARB	-.030	.190	-.168	.097	.083	.028	-.124	.036	60
CELA	-.067	-.076	.147	-.046	.229	-.120	-.098	.155	60
CENM	-.108	.088	.111	.007	.174	.072	-.082	.066	60
CERM	-.024	-.033	-.105	.017	.054	.071	.017	.062	60
CRIS	-.160	.097	.002	-.041	.078	-.109	-.075	.048	60
DIAN	-.316*	.038	-.039	-.022	-.046	-.014	-.028	-.036	60
EATO	.182	-.016	.015	.093	.157	-.109	-.189	-.052	60
ECAT	-.085	.137	-.057	.036	-.014	.028	-.056	-.021	60
FRIS	.158	-.210	.224	.238	.123	.129	-.051	.069	60
FUND	.041	-.063	-.004	.017	.168	-.132	-.017	.112	60
GESA	-.022	-.037	-.148	.058	.211	-.102	-.026	.075	60
IEM	-.044	-.003	-.214	.081	.140	-.028	-.130	.132	60

TABLE IV.12 (CONTINUED)

****

STOCK	1	2	3	4	5	6	7	8	T
INDE	-.057	.009	.046	.083	.056	-.074	-.045	-.088	60
KIMB	-.138	-.083	-.034	-.074	.260	-.105	-.014	.053	60
LAMO	-.211	.162	.175	-.223	-.032	-.104	-.210	.144	60
LIVE	-.118	-.254	.240	-.136	.084	.105	-.020	.040	60
LORE	.062	-.192	-.068	.210	.052	-.100	-.006	.189	60
LUIS	.041	.138	-.078	-.038	-.060	.094	-.060	.010	60
MODE	.124	-.295*	-.086	.076	-.011	-.269	-.151	.239	60
MORE	.384*	.233	.136	.214	.213	.019	-.018	-.081	60
NAFI	.054	-.019	.152	-.203	-.221	.251	.031	-.054	60
NEGR	-.029	-.037	.032	-.059	.259	.083	-.047	.065	60
PALA	-.101	-.118	-.060	.137	.052	.095	-.023	-.050	60
PENO	-.337*	-.041	-.166	.245	-.060	-.096	.054	.034	60
SANB	-.062	.162	.272*	-.080	.144	.122	.030	.082	60
SPIC	-.027	-.000	.084	-.132	.344*	-.177	-.107	.052	60
TAMS	.026	-.114	.052	-.047	.138	-.121	-.076	.072	60
TREM	.021	.043	-.149	-.037	.078	-.104	-.219	-.077	60

****

* Sample autocorrelation is at least two standard errors to the left or or to the right of its expected value under the hypothesis that the true autocorrelation is zero.

If the return series has been generated by a white noise, the sample autocorrelation coefficients for L > 0 are approximately distributed according to a normal distribution with mean zero and standard deviation 1/sq.root of T. Thus, if a stock has 60 observations, one can assign a standard error of .129 to the first autocorrelation coefficient. Then, if the first autocorrelation coefficient was greater than .258 one would be 95% sure that the true autocorrelation coefficient is not zero.

TABLE IV.13

SAMPLE AUTOCORRELATIONS FOR MONTHLY REAL
RETURNS ON 37 MEXICAN STOCKS FOR LAGS L=1,2...8
1977-1981

STOCK	1	2	3	4	5	6	7	8	T
ACEY	-.025	.186	.083	.259	.043	.071	.100	-.079	60
ALUM	-.218	.067	.121	-.024	.059	-.191	.052	-.016	60
APAS	-.135	-.047	.200	-.085	.153	-.074	.040	-.065	60
AVIA	.374*	.173	.155	-.064	.033	.061	-.015	.054	60
BACA	-.016	.093	-.151	.012	-.121	.118	-.107	.122	60
BANA	.086	-.029	.056	-.061	.123	.174	-.053	.079	60
BCH	-.485*	.365*	-.157	.028	-.035	.128	-.190	.162	60
CAMP	.030	.001	.081	-.134	-.127	.008	-.098	-.097	60
CANN	.107	.205	.119	.113	.160	.055	.167	.069	60
CARB	-.041	.172	.003	.141	-.093	.070	.008	.148	60
CELA	.027	.167	.171	.068	.037	.085	.206	.022	60
CENM	-.024	-.081	.309*	-.132	.069	.214	-.008	.056	60
CERM	-.103	.126	.114	.016	.045	.030	.169	.065	60
CRIS	.066	.267*	.043	.063	.143	.103	.126	.066	60
DIAN	-.046	-.093	-.081	-.040	-.098	.078	.098	.158	60
EATO	.004	-.004	.099	.081	.138	.066	-.147	-.082	60
ECAT	.151	-.011	.077	-.126	.022	-.020	-.046	-.094	60
FRIS	.281*	.181	-.020	.067	-.006	-.109	-.064	-.046	60
FUND	.051	-.017	-.008	-.030	-.130	.088	.056	-.137	60
GESA	-.007	.245	.167	-.041	-.074	.139	-.027	.005	60
IEM	.002	-.041	.359*	-.017	-.100	-.053	.096	.088	60

TABLE IV.13 (CONTINUED)

STOCK	1	2	3	4	5	6	7	8	T
INDE	-.071	.074	-.032	.189	.082	-.049	-.196	.193	60
KIMB	-.200	-.007	.044	.016	.012	.071	.019	.073	60
LAMO	.067	.285*	.135	.241	.153	-.011	.205	.163	60
LIVE	.232	.113	.285*	.096	.080	.208	.022	-.015	60
LORE	-.011	.031	.022	-.274*	-.095	-.011	.178	.166	60
LUIS	-.057	-.057	.059	-.024	.066	-.054	-.059	.079	60
MODE	.239	.119	.137	.196	.017	.059	.206	.075	60
MORE	.039	.124	.106	-.047	-.124	.096	-.222	.053	60
NAFI	.288*	.243	.050	.007	-.043	-.315*	-.065	-.142	60
NEGR	-.043	.049	-.048	.092	-.088	-.060	-.023	-.092	60
PALA	.189	.146	.096	.063	.125	-.081	-.116	-.024	60
PENO	.098	.081	.063	.028	.317*	-.047	-.104	-.019	60
SANB	.172	.011	.011	-.044	.022	.071	.035	-.090	60
SPIC	.214	-.009	.053	.134	.026	-.013	-.010	.074	60
TAMS	.085	.169	.047	.140	.182	.020	-.067	.209	60
TREM	.050	.335*	.299*	.161	.066	.070	.087	-.096	60

* Sample autocorrelation is at least two standard errors to the left or to the right of its expected value under the hypothesis that the true autocorrelation is zero.
If the return series has been generated by a white noise, the sample autocorrelation coefficients for L > 0 are approximately distributed according to a normal distribution with mean zero and standard deviation 1/sq.root of T. Thus, if a stock has 60 observations, one can assign a standard error of .129 to the first autocorrelation coefficient. Then, if the first autocorrelation coefficient was greater than .258 one would be 95% sure that the true autocorrelation coefficient is not zero.

TABLE IV.14

SAMPLE AUTOCORRELATIONS ON MONTHLY PORTFOLIO
REAL RETURNS FOR LAGS L=1,2,..8
1972-1981

****

PORT	1	2	3	4	5	6	7	8	T
Port. 1	.286*	.220*	.158	.034	.144	-.011	.022	.071	120
Port. 2	.175	.151	.083	.026	.036	.072	.004	.183	120
Port. 3	.208*	.285*	.295*	.167	.110	.114*	-.024	.151	120
Port. 4	.199*	.033	.150	.056	.023	.041	.009	.033	120
Port. 5	.110	.006	.156	.070	.129	-.046	-.028	.050	120

****

* Significant at the 95% confidence level.

TABLE IV.15

SAMPLE AUTOCORRELATIONS ON MONTHLY PORTFOLIO
REAL RETURNS FOR LAGS L=1,2,..8
1972-1976

PORT	1	2	3	4	5	6	7	8	T
Port. 1	.055	-.082	.218	-.021	.191	-.085	-.288	.172	60
Port. 2	.116	-.013	.068	.103	.282	-.050	-.161	.096	60
Port. 3	.105	.227	.194	.049	.282	-.029	-.081	.088	60
Port. 4	-.015	-.156	-.005	.149	.043	.002	-.073	.011	60
Port. 5	-.006	-.255	-.069	.073	.230	-.141	-.112	.037	60

TABLE IV.16

SAMPLE AUTOCORRELATIONS ON MONTHLY PORTFOLIO
REAL RETURNS FOR LAGS L=1,2,...8
1977-1981

****

PORT	1	2	3	4	5	6	7	8	T
Port. 1	.325*	.274	.119	.015	.114	-.039	.070	.027	60
Port. 2	.185	.193	.062	-.021	-.059	.110	.060	.170	60
Port. 3	.231	.296*	.307*	.190	.039	.147	.009	.144	60
Port. 4	.324*	.148	.227	.001	.039	.063	.055	.051	60
Port. 5	.182	.163	.260	.068	.118	-.039	.035	.020	60

****

* Significant at the 95% confidence level.

TABLE IV.17

THE MARKET MODEL
Ri = C + B Rm + Ei
1972-1981

****

Ri	C	T(C)	B	T(B)	ADJ. R*2	D-W	F-STAT	T
ACEY	.005	0.349	0.858	3.879	.1056	2.147	15.050	120
ALUM	.009	0.842	0.493	3.215	.0727	2.560 (A)	10.336	120
APAS	.013	1.018	1.251	6.744	.2721	2.462 (A)	45.482	120
AVIA	.015	1.170	1.416	7.608	.3234	1.955	57.882	120
BACA	.003	0.183	0.859	4.168	.1209	2.218	17.372	120
BANA	.012	1.427	0.697	5.544	.1999	2.466 (A)	30.740	120
BCH	.013	1.036	0.667	3.440	.0835	2.770 (A)	11.836	120
CAMP	-.010	-0.578	1.287	5.186	.1787	2.055	26.894	120
CANN	.027	1.851	0.818	3.681	.0954	2.095	13.551	120
CARB	-.002	-0.312	1.031	8.610	.3807	2.388 (A)	74.141	120
CELA	-.005	-0.765	1.163	12.265	.5567	2.638 (A)	150.431	120
CENM	-.002	-0.226	0.786	6.399	.2513	2.270	40.949	120
CERM	-.008	-0.875	1.404	10.301	.4690	2.528 (A)	106.102	120
CRIS	.002	0.146	1.054	6.252	.2424	2.391 (A)	39.084	120
DIAN	.012	0.564	0.866	2.612	.0467	2.540 (A)	6.825	120
EATO	.007	0.623	1.284	7.510	.3177	1.905	56.401	120
ECAT	-.006	-0.367	1.089	4.374	.1322	2.078	19.133	120
FRIS	.005	0.483	1.061	6.250	.2424	1.685	39.068	120
FUND	-.008	-0.611	0.633	3.276	.0756	1.920	10.731	120
GESA	.004	0.347	0.586	3.809	.1019	2.451 (A)	14.509	120
IEM	.005	0.330	0.499	2.354	.0368	2.181	5.542	120

TABLE IV.17 (CONTINUED)

****

Ri	C	T(C)	B	T(B)	ADJ. R*2	D-W	F-STAT	T
INDE	.013	1.093	0.791	4.540	.1415	2.313	20.611	120
KIMB	.010	1.013	1.218	8.218	.3586	2.699 (A)	67.539	120
LAMO	.013	1.318	0.690	4.761	.1540	2.522 (A)	22.668	120
LIVE	.009	1.249	0.572	5.291	.1849	1.943	27.991	120
LORE	-.005	-0.371	0.951	4.539	.1415	2.004	20.607	120
LUIS	.030	2.423	0.748	4.077	.1160	2.278	16.622	120
MODE	-.007	-0.675	1.116	7.305	.3056	1.847	53.366	120
MORE	.015	1.421	0.970	6.053	.2305	2.085	36.642	120
NAFI	.001	0.227	0.650	6.646	.2662	1.735	44.171	120
NEGR	.015	2.313	0.348	3.467	.0847	2.300	12.017	120
PALA	.014	1.841	0.623	5.493	.1969	2.296	30.169	120
PENO	.014	1.237	0.870	5.014	.1687	2.270	25.144	120
SANB	.011	1.177	0.624	4.406	.1340	1.905	19.415	120
SPIC	.014	1.688	1.011	8.404	.3691	2.136	70.625	120
TAMS	.027	2.542	0.535	3.305	.0770	2.135	10.926	120
TREM	-.001	-0.108	1.104	6.718	.2705	2.455 (A)	45.135	120

****

The five percent significance points for DW test are dl=1.65 and du=1.69. Then,
(A) 2.35 < DW < 4.00   Reject null hypothesis that p=0; negative s. c. present.
(B) 2.31 < DW < 2.35   Result indeterminate.
(C) 2.00 < DW < 2.31   Accept null hypothesis.
(D) 1.69 < DW < 2.00   Accept null hypothesis.
(E) 1.65 < DW < 1.69   Result indeterminate.
(F) 0.00 < DW < 1.65   Reject null hypothesis that p=0; positive s. c. present.

TABLE IV.18

THE MARKET MODEL
Rp = C + B Rm + Ep
1972-1981

****

Rp	C	T(C)	B	T(B)	ADJ. R*2	D-W	F-STAT	T
Port. 1	.009	1.873	0.815	11.552	.5268	2.431 (A)	133.457	120
Port. 2	.006	1.220	0.854	11.439	.5218	2.213	130.849	120
Port. 3	.006	1.137	0.953	12.932	.5828	2.525 (A)	167.228	120
Port. 4	.007	1.417	0.990	12.595	.5698	2.568 (A)	158.632	120
Port. 5	.007	1.546	0.761	10.770	.4914	2.651 (A)	115.995	120

****

The five percent significance points for DW test are dl=1.65 and du=1.69. Then,
(A) 2.35 < DW < 4.00 Reject null hypothesis that p=0; negative s. c. present.
(B) 2.31 < DW < 2.35 Result indeterminate.
(C) 2.00 < DW < 2.31 Accept null hypothesis.
(D) 1.69 < DW < 2.00 Accept null hypothesis.
(E) 1.65 < DW < 1.69 Result indeterminate.
(F) 0.00 < DW < 1.65 Reject null hypothesis that p=0; positive s. c. present.

TABLE IV.19

TESTING HETEROSCEDASTICITY ON
THE MARKET MODEL
$|ei| = a + b RMi + wi$

****

IeI	a	T(a)	b	T(b)
ACEY	.103	10.480	0.435	2.945 (B)
ALUM	.076	10.452	-0.139	-1.263
APAS	.079	8.731	0.357	2.640 (B)
AVIA	.083	8.917	0.161	1.150
BACA	.097	10.148	0.275	1.921
BANA	.055	8.851	0.147	1.574
BCH	.085	8.392	-0.017	-0.110
CAMP	.113	9.714	0.407	2.333 (B)
CANN	.099	9.119	0.257	1.572
CARB	.061	11.449	0.037	0.460
CELA	.043	10.097	0.214	3.345 (B)
CENM	.060	10.538	0.031	0.365
CERM	.067	10.488	-0.003	-0.033
CRIS	.079	9.498	-0.063	-0.504
DIAN	.103	5.181	-0.016	-0.054
EATO	.084	11.221	0.268	2.395 (B)
ECAT	.118	10.665	0.458	2.765 (B)
FRIS	.086	11.424	0.080	0.708
FUND	.092	9.754	-0.017	-0.121
GESA	.067	8.438	0.033	0.275
IEM	.097	9.433	0.215	1.397

TABLE IV.19 (CONTINUED)

****

|e|	a	T(a)	b	T(b)
INDE	.082	10.116	0.187	1.535
KIMB	.063	8.304	0.163	1.435
LAMO	.059	7.997	0.260	2.357 (B)
LIVE	.054	10.743	0.011	0.153
LORE	.082	7.186	0.141	0.828
LUIS	.092	11.280	0.161	1.316
MODE	.069	9.793	0.279	2.628 (B)
MORE	.083	11.472	-0.035	-0.324
NAFI	.044	9.133	0.117	1.631
NEGR	.049	10.055	-0.077	-1.055
PALA	.054	10.042	0.048	0.598
PENO	.088	11.104	0.003	0.027
SANB	.067	9.681	0.036	0.345
SPIC	.060	12.244	0.224	3.018 (B)
TAMS	.080	10.573	0.068	0.603
TREM	.078	9.708	0.042	0.350

****

This test using the absolute values of the residuals was proposed by Glejser (JASA,1969). Two relevant possibilities may arise:(A) If the estimated intercept does not differ significantly from zero whereas the estimated slope does :heteroscedasticity is present and we have to deflate the original equation by RMi. (B) If both, the estimated intercept and slope are significantly different from zero: heteroscedasticity is present and we have to deflate by (a+bRMi). Finally, in all the other cases, the hypothesis of homoscedasticity is accepted.

TABLE IV.20

TESTING HETEROSCEDASTICITY ON
THE MARKET MODEL

IepI = a + b RMp + wp

****

IeI	a	T(a)	b	T(b)
Port. 1	.037	11.084	0.019	0.380
Port. 2	.037	11.156	0.078	1.562
Port. 3	.037	11.161	0.081	1.645
Port. 4	.034	8.811	0.120	2.076 (B)
Port. 5	.034	9.072	-0.054	-1.045

****

This test using the absolute values of the residuals was proposed by Glejser (JASA,1969). Two relevant possibilities may arise:(A) If the estimated intercept does not differ significantly from zero whereas the estimated slope does :heteroscedasticity is present and we have to deflate the original equation by RMi. (B) If both, the estimated intercept and slope are significantly different from zero: heteroscedasticity is present and we have to deflate by (a+bRMi). Finally, in all the other cases, the hypothesis of homoscedasticity is accepted.

TABLE IV.21

THE MARKET MODEL CORRECTED
FOR SERIAL CORRELATION *
INDIVIDUAL SHARES
1972-1981

****

Ri	C	T(C)	B	T(B)	ADJ. R*2	D-W	F-STAT	T
ALUM	.008	1.020	0.540	4.141	.1204	2.059	17.152	119
BANA	.009	1.486	0.851	7.896	.3421	2.041	62.350	119
BCH	.015	1.790	0.543	3.613	.0927	1.795	13.057	119
CARB	-.002	-0.234	1.007	9.262	.4181	1.938	85.779	119
CERM	-.006	-0.917	1.336	11.553	.5289	1.975	133.464	119
CRIS	.001	0.065	1.141	7.450	.3160	1.985	55.509	119
DIAN	.012	0.722	0.931	3.293	.0770	1.988	10.841	119
GESA	.000	0.058	0.753	5.688	.2099	1.905	32.352	119
KIMB	.012	1.729	1.147	9.796	.4459	2.042	95.968	119
TREM	-.003	-0.310	1.184	7.966	.3461	2.034	63.450	119

****

* The correction for first-order serial correlation of the error term was performed using the Hildreth-Lu grid technique.

TABLE IV.22

THE MARKET MODEL CORRECTED
FOR SERIAL CORRELATION *
PORTFOLIOS
1972-1981

****

Rp	C	T(C)	B	T(B)	ADJ. R*2	D-W	F-STAT	T
PORT. 1	.008	2.066	0.910	13.667	.6115	2.081	186.790	119
PORT. 3	.005	1.309	0.996	15.795	.6780	1.790	249.496	119
PORT. 5	.006	1.841	0.797	13.515	.6062	2.206	182.642	119

****

* The correction for first-order serial correlation of the error term was performed using the Hildreth-Lu grid technique.

TABLE IV.23

THE MARKET MODEL CORRECTED
FOR HETEROSCEDASTICITY

$$\frac{Ri}{(a+bRm)} = \frac{C}{(a+bRm)} + B^* \frac{Rm}{(a+bRm)} + \frac{Ei}{(a+bRm)}$$

$$Y^* = C^* + B^* X^* + E^*$$

****

Y^*	C^*	$T(C^*)$	B^*	$T(B^*)$
ACEY	.003	0.195	1.135	5.718
CAMP	-.009	-0.614	1.237	5.352
EATO	.007	0.654	1.329	8.145
ECAT	-.003	-0.188	0.800	3.594
MODE	-.006	-0.668	1.085	7.418
SPIC	.014	1.780	1.030	8.701

****

TABLE IV.24

THE MARKET MODEL CORRECTED FOR HETEROSCEDASTICITY
AND SERIAL CORRELATION

****

STOCK	C	T(C)	B	T(B)
APAS	.003	0.227	1.139	5.710
CELA	.007	0.896	0.546	4.749
LAMO	.012	1.251	1.338	8.506
PORT.4	.007	2.046	1.019	16.093

****

TABLE IV.25

THE MARKET MODEL CORRECTED FOR SERIAL
CORRELATION AND HETEROSCEDASTICITY

****

STOCK	C	T(C)	B	T(B)
APAS	.003	0.238	1.087	5.281
CELA	.008	0.761	0.554	3.377
LAMO	.012	1.040	1.315	7.387
PORT.4	.007	1.507	0.970	13.063

****

TABLE IV.26

THE CAPITAL ASSET PRICING MODEL

Ri- Rf = C + B (Rm -Rf) + Ei

1972-198

Ri	C	T(C)	B	T(B)	ADJ. R*2	D-W	F-STAT	T
ACEY	.003	0.157	1.009	6.125	.2348	2.146	37.512	120
ALUM	-.042	-2.707	0.606	5.338	.1877	2.592 (A)	28.499	120
APAS	.027	1.435	1.094	7.884	.3394	2.439 (A)	62.163	120
AVIA	.059	3.160	1.352	9.832	.4457	1.971	96.670	120
BACA	-.030	-1.448	0.716	4.732	.1524	2.261	22.393	120
BANA	-.010	-0.815	0.838	8.848	.3938	2.519 (A)	78.289	120
BCH	-.033	-1.698	0.617	4.353	.1311	2.886 (A)	18.953	120
CAMP	.003	0.106	1.068	5.755	.2125	2.039	33.119	120
CANN	.010	0.467	0.869	5.252	.1826	2.104	27.589	120
CARB	-.001	-0.087	1.008	11.319	.5165	2.392 (A)	128.115	120
CELA	.009	0.993	1.109	15.693	.6733	2.639 (A)	246.263	120
CENM	-.015	-1.209	0.910	9.868	.4475	2.223	97.375	120
CERM	.029	2.106	1.285	12.622	.5709	2.556 (A)	159.310	120
CRIS	.013	0.771	1.100	8.789	.3905	2.417 (A)	77.250	120
DIAN	.007	0.224	0.976	3.956	.1096	2.543 (A)	15.650	120
EATO	.021	1.183	1.080	8.407	.3693	1.901	70.678	120
ECAT	-.004	-0.155	1.006	5.426	.1929	2.071	29.438	120
FRIS	.019	1.145	1.124	8.934	.3985	1.709	79.825	120
FUND	-.046	-2.363	0.700	4.882	.1610	1.940	23.836	120
GESA	-.023	-1.482	0.814	6.978	.2861	2.499 (A)	48.692	120
IEM	-.043	-2.007	0.631	3.995	.1117	2.228	15.960	120

TABLE IV.26 (CONTINUED)

****

Ri	C	T(C)	B	T(B)	ADJ. R*2	D-W	F-STAT	T
INDE	.003	0.177	0.945	7.252	.3024	2.314	52.590	120
KIMB	.027	1.805	1.125	10.169	.4625	2.701 (A)	103.408	120
LAMO	-.007	-0.501	0.861	7.884	.3395	2.507 (A)	62.161	120
LIVE	-.022	-1.958	0.777	9.351	.4208	1.888	87.449	120
LORE	-.014	-0.658	0.925	5.943	.2238	2.009	35.317	120
LUIS	.012	0.651	0.875	6.386	.2505	2.291	40.776	120
MODE	.007	0.460	1.114	9.814	.4447	1.853	96.308	120
MORE	.009	0.561	0.946	7.939	.3427	2.084	63.034	120
NAFI	-.034	-3.535	0.716	9.938	.4510	1.785	98.771	120
NEGR	-.045	-4.382	0.534	7.057	.2908	2.346	49.798	120
PALA	-.016	-1.335	0.783	9.107	.4078	2.361	82.939	120
PENO	.006	0.315	0.938	7.261	.3029	2.265	52.717	120
SANB	-.026	-1.860	0.705	6.718	.2705	1.931	45.129	120
SPIC	.014	1.124	0.999	11.150	.5089	2.134	124.331	120
TAMS	-.004	-0.267	0.775	6.303	.2455	2.186	39.726	120
TREM	.013	0.794	1.119	9.172	.4112	2.470 (A)	84.122	120

****

The five percent significance points for DW test are dl=1.65 and du=1.69. Then,
(A) 2.35 < DW < 4.00 Reject null hypothesis that p=0; negative s. c. present.
(B) 2.31 < DW < 2.35 Result indeterminate.
(C) 2.00 < DW < 2.31 Accept null hypothesis.
(D) 1.69 < DW < 2.00 Accept null hypothesis.
(E) 1.65 < DW < 1.69 Result indeterminate.
(F) 0.00 < DW < 1.65 Reject null hypothesis that p=0; positive s. c. present.

TABLE IV.27

THE CAPITAL ASSET PRICING MODEL
Rp- Rf = C + B (Rm -Rf) + Ep
1972-1981

****

Rp	C	T(C)	B	T(B)	ADJ. R*2	D-W	F-STAT	T
Port. 1	-.005	-0.651	0.891	16.251	.6886	2.477 (A)	264.105	120
Port. 2	-.009	-1.164	0.883	15.931	.6799	2.234	253.798	120
Port. 3	.003	0.398	0.983	17.892	.7284	2.537 (A)	320.139	120
Port. 4	.007	0.826	0.993	16.980	.7071	2.570 (A)	288.332	120
Port. 5	-.013	-1.758	0.850	15.955	.6806	2.646 (A)	254.559	120

****

The five percent significance points for DW test are dl=1.65 and du=1.69. Then,
(A) 2.35 < DW < 4.00 Reject null hypothesis that p=0; negative s. c. present.
(B) 2.31 < DW < 2.35 Result indeterminate.
(C) 2.00 < DW < 2.31 Accept null hypothesis.
(D) 1.69 < DW < 2.00 Accept null hypothesis.
(E) 1.65 < DW < 1.69 Result indeterminate.
(F) 0.00 < DW < 1.65 Reject null hypothesis that p=0; positive s. c. present.

TABLE IV.28

TESTING HETEROSCEDASTICITY
ON THE C.A.P.M.

IEiI = a + b (Rm -Rf) + wi

IEiI	a	T(a)	b	T(b)
ACEY	.139	9.169	0.264	2.366 (B)
ALUM	.060	5.627	-0.142	-1.786
APAS	.097	6.835	0.110	1.053
AVIA	.094	6.757	0.092	0.887
BACA	.095	6.581	-0.045	-0.417
BANA	.068	7.175	0.096	1.364
BCH	.058	3.979	-0.250	-2.328 (B)
CAMP	.152	8.597	0.311	2.373 (B)
CANN	.123	7.437	0.187	1.532
CARB	.064	7.979	0.025	0.411
CELA	.059	8.988	0.121	2.486 (B)
CENM	.056	6.417	-0.053	-0.825
CERM	.061	6.190	-0.054	-0.737
CRIS	.064	5.134	-0.136	-1.477
DIAN	.105	3.504	0.017	0.078
EATO	.108	9.358	0.182	2.140 (B)
ECAT	.162	9.748	0.350	2.837 (B)
FRIS	.090	7.972	0.025	0.299
FUND	.072	5.209	-0.193	-1.884
GESA	.060	4.995	-0.090	-1.010
IEM	.110	7.004	0.094	0.814

TABLE IV.28 (CONTINUED)

****

IEiI	a	T(a)	b	T(b)
INDE	.087	6.929	0.008	0.088
KIMB	.074	6.423	0.084	0.988
LAMO	.078	6.945	0.120	1.442
LIVE	.050	6.224	-0.042	-0.709
LORE	.071	4.164	-0.118	-0.932
LUIS	.105	8.349	0.099	1.066
MODE	.088	8.089	0.125	1.562
MORE	.071	6.561	-0.113	-1.417
NAFI	.043	6.006	-0.022	-0.407
NEGR	.041	5.569	-0.081	-1.507
PALA	.046	5.686	-0.111	-1.861
PENO	.079	6.612	-0.088	-1.007
SANB	.064	6.141	-0.026	-0.339
SPIC	.071	9.237	0.064	1.132
TAMS	.076	6.608	-0.059	-0.693
TREM	.082	6.805	0.030	0.334

****

This test using the absolute values of the residuals was proposed by Glejser (JASA,1969). Two relevant possibilities may arise:(A) If the estimated intercept does not differ significantly from zero whereas the estimated slope does :heteroscedasticity is present and we have to deflate the original equation by RMi. (B) If both, the estimated intercept and slope are significantly different from zero: heteroscedasticity is present and we have to deflate by (a+bRMi). Finally, in all the other cases, the hypothesis of homoscedasticity is accepted.

TABLE IV.29

TESTING HETEROSCEDASTICITY
ON THE C.A.P.M.

$IEpI = a + b (Rm - Rf) + wp$

****

IEpI	a	T(a)	b	T(b)
Port. 1	.038	7.477	0.002	0.063
Port. 2	.037	7.277	-0.009	-0.248
Port. 3	.039	7.834	0.012	0.313
Port. 4	.046	7.918	0.095	2.198 (B)
Port. 5	.029	5.622	-0.044	-1.149

****

This test using the absolute values of the residuals was proposed by Glejser (JASA,1969). Two relevant possibilities may arise:(A) If the estimated intercept does not differ significantly from zero whereas the estimated slope does :heteroscedasticity is present and we have to deflate the original equation by RMi. (B) If both, the estimated intercept and slope are significantly different from zero: heteroscedasticity is present and we have to deflate by (a+bRMi). Finally, in all the other cases, the hypothesis of homoscedasticity is accepted.

TABLE IV.30

THE C. A. P. M. CORRECTED
FOR SERIAL CORRELATION *
INDIVIDUAL SHARES
1972-1981

Ri	C	T(C)	B	T(B)	ADJ. R*2	D-W	F-STAT	T
ALUM	-.037	-3.111	0.659	7.225	.3025	2.111	52.196	119
APAS	.025	1.555	1.074	8.974	.4026	2.071	80.525	119
BANA	-.000	-0.017	0.934	12.374	.5631	2.072	153.126	119
CARB	-.002	-0.182	0.996	12.917	.5843	1.940	166.861	119
CERM	.024	2.259	1.232	15.279	.6633	2.009	233.439	119
CRIS	.019	1.302	1.149	10.633	.4871	2.006	113.060	119
DIAN	.013	0.490	1.019	5.173	.1792	1.990	26.765	119
GESA	-.012	-0.959	0.925	9.914	.4519	1.952	98.279	119
KIMB	.022	2.063	1.073	13.283	.5979	2.053	176.448	119
LAMO	-.002	-0.193	0.908	10.357	.4738	1.864	107.263	119
TREM	.017	1.230	1.159	11.040	.5060	2.037	121.882	119

* The correction for first-order serial correlation of the error term was performed using the Hildreth-Lu grid technique.

TABLE IV.31

THE C. A. P. M. CORRECTED
FOR SERIAL CORRELATION *
PORTFOLIOS
1972-1981

****

Rp	C	T(C)	B	T(B)	ADJ. R*2	D-W	F-STAT	T
Port. 1	-.000	-0.010	0.935	21.208	.7918	1.918	449.770	119
Port. 3	.006	0.954	1.007	22.925	.8164	1.796	525.537	119
Port. 5	-.010	-1.733	0.882	21.138	.7907	2.188	446.813	119

****

* The correction for first-order serial correlation of the error term was performed using the Hildreth-Lu grid technique.

TABLE IV.32

THE C.A.P.M. CORRECTED
FOR HETEROSCEDASTICITY

$$\frac{Ri-Rf}{[a+b(Rm-Rf)]} = \frac{C}{[a+b(Rm-Rf)]} + B* \frac{Rm-Rf}{[a+b(Rm-Rf)]} + \frac{Ei}{[a+b(Rm-Rf)]}$$

$$Y* = C* + B* X* + E*$$

****

Y*	C*	T(C*)	B*	T(B*)
ACEY	.014	0.591	1.103	8.161
CAMP	-.043	-3.466	0.595	5.516
EATO	.026	1.305	1.089	8.317
ECAT	.061	3.128	1.371	10.654

****

TABLE IV.33

THE C.A.P.M. CORRECTED FOR HETEROSCEDASTICITY
AND SERIAL CORRELATION

****

STOCK	C	T(C)	B	T(B)
BCH	.015	0.624	1.107	8.136
CELA	-.038	-3.998	0.642	7.445
PORT.4	.007	1.109	1.000	27.941

****

TABLE IV.34

THE C.A.P.M. CORRECTED FOR SERIAL
CORRELATION AND HETEROSCEDASTICITY
****
STOCK	C	T(C)	B	T(B)
BCH	.017	0.681	1.119	8.442
CELA	-.041	-2.064	0.614	5.730
PORT.4	.005	0.531	0.981	21.423
****

TABLE IV.35

SELECTED STOCKS AND TRANSACTION DAYS
(521 WEDNESDAYS)

STOCK	1972	1973	1974	1975	1976	1977	1978	1979	1980	1981	TOTAL
ACCO	6	8	12	12	17	5	22	32	18	15	147
ACEY	9	14	4	19	31	17	41	50	45	43	273
ALUM	36	37	28	34	46	46	48	50	48	27	400
APAS	27	25	30	18	13	30	35	42	49	52	321
AVIA	16	24	22	31	47	48	52	52	51	50	393
BACA	36	33	33	25	15	25	41	45	40	29	322
BANA	45	40	39	42	53	51	52	52	52	53	479
BIME	11	8	19	8	11	3	39	50	41	43	233
CAMP	32	46	38	20	35	26	41	52	48	39	377
CANN	44	39	33	30	29	16	43	51	51	41	377
CARB	42	49	41	39	47	50	50	51	50	44	463
CELA	46	52	46	46	46	46	52	52	52	52	490
CENM	25	24	13	17	11	13	33	29	36	25	226
CERM	33	35	28	31	28	24	47	52	52	53	383
CRIS	13	18	16	18	4	13	52	52	52	51	289
EATO	33	35	39	30	38	31	48	50	48	45	397
ECAT	16	10	9	12	16	8	17	46	25	18	177
FRIS	4	33	37	21	19	26	38	52	52	53	335
FUND	47	50	51	47	42	28	49	50	45	48	457
GESA	22	9	9	6	20	24	29	15	18	9	161
IEM	21	25	25	24	29	12	40	31	17	18	242
INDE	16	17	19	11	22	15	17	26	17	12	172

TABLE IV.35 (CONTINUED)

STOCK	1972	1973	1974	1975	1976	1977	1978	1979	1980	1981	TOTAL
KIMB	31	47	43	47	50	52	52	52	52	53	479
LAMO	13	14	5	6	5	2	19	20	8	11	103
LIVE	50	46	43	45	45	45	52	52	52	51	481
LORE	4	10	9	11	9	5	22	39	44	34	187
LUIS	2	27	34	24	30	39	52	52	51	53	364
NEGR	36	27	24	23	25	19	23	18	7	9	211
PALA	30	32	27	11	11	11	24	25	22	28	221
PENO	28	43	43	33	36	44	49	51	52	53	432
SANB	25	30	30	21	37	31	47	51	47	49	368
SPIC	34	36	30	29	36	38	49	49	38	39	378
TAMS	24	37	34	29	36	12	33	51	42	44	342
TREM	11	20	12	9	5	1	49	52	46	47	250

TABLE IV.36

SCHOLES-WILLIAM BETA
INDIVIDUAL MONTHLY RETURNS

$$Ri = C + B1\ Rm(-2) + B2\ Rm(-1) + B3\ Rm + B4\ Rm(1) + B5\ Rm(2) + Ei$$

****

Ri	C	T(C)	B1	T(B1)	B2	T(B2)	B3	T(B3)
ACEY	.005	0.284	.188	0.778	-.088	-0.353	0.884	3.600
ALUM	.007	0.634	.009	0.053	.175	0.979	0.423	2.419
APAS	.016	1.159	.041	0.200	.021	0.099	1.266	6.013
AVIA	.008	0.619	.194	1.011	-.076	-0.384	1.296	6.661
BACA	.002	0.177	-.718	-3.433	.219	1.009	0.723	3.398
BANA	.007	0.830	-.038	-0.303	.132	1.001	0.494	3.824
BCH	.013	0.990	-.196	-1.000	-.130	-0.636	0.738	3.700
CAMP	-.010	-0.589	-.400	-1.612	.081	0.313	1.255	4.972
CANN	.022	1.399	.306	1.255	.041	0.161	0.671	2.708
CARB	.001	0.162	.063	0.488	-.347	-2.572	1.104	8.360
CELA	-.002	-0.357	.045	0.428	-.025	-0.225	1.201	11.133
CENM	.004	0.444	-.132	-0.967	.025	0.179	0.859	6.192
CERM	-.003	-0.263	.217	1.482	-.178	-1.167	1.513	10.144
CRIS	-.007	-0.573	.225	1.224	.161	0.845	0.873	4.679
DIAN	.016	0.654	-.471	-1.278	.110	0.288	0.801	2.138
EATO	.012	0.915	-.014	-0.075	-.104	-0.523	1.357	6.996
ECAT	-.006	-0.321	.018	0.064	.310	1.080	1.039	3.697
FRIS	.001	0.094	.035	0.184	.162	0.823	0.946	4.899
FUND	-.013	-0.944	-.187	-0.901	.124	0.574	0.557	2.644

TABLE IV.36 (CONTINUED)

Ri	C	T(C)	B1	T(B1)	B2	T(B2)	B3	T(B3)
GESA	-.005	-0.504	.186	1.146	.354	2.096	0.342	2.072
IEM	-.011	-0.762	-.057	-0.253	.595	2.540	0.178	0.776
INDE	.008	0.651	-.080	-0.427	-.095	-0.484	0.708	3.700
KIMB	.018	1.679	-.078	-0.479	-.281	-1.670	1.339	8.124
LAMO	.009	0.872	.356	2.300	-.157	-0.976	0.611	3.882
LIVE	.010	1.344	.011	0.096	.025	0.208	0.555	4.631
LORE	.005	0.318	-.389	-1.693	-.075	-0.316	1.099	4.708
LUIS	.025	1.910	-.200	-1.020	.163	0.802	0.614	3.076
MODE	-.010	-0.845	.068	0.400	-.110	-0.623	1.074	6.189
MORE	.014	1.181	-.208	-1.174	.330	1.794	0.880	4.888
NAFI	-.000	-0.042	.069	0.635	.101	0.889	0.596	5.371
NEGR	.013	1.942	.026	0.248	.384	3.518	0.273	2.549
PALA	.007	0.989	-.137	-1.287	.439	3.967	0.431	3.977
PENO	.021	1.672	-.253	-1.349	.096	0.495	0.896	4.693
SANB	.015	1.477	-.138	-0.905	-.243	-1.540	0.626	4.046
SPIC	.016	1.914	.082	0.641	.115	0.868	0.987	7.611
TAMS	.021	1.820	.048	0.280	.232	1.303	0.301	1.727
TREM	-.011	-0.965	.141	0.793	.388	2.099	0.930	5.138

TABLE IV.36 (CONT)

Ri	B4	T(B4)	B5	T(B5)	ADJ.R*2	D-W	F-STAT	T	S-W BETA*
ACEY	-.098	-0.398	.100	0.426	.0898	2.147	3.269	116	0.931
ALUM	.096	0.551	-.118	-0.707	.0531	2.561	2.290	116	0.589
APAS	.056	0.267	-.209	-1.036	.2601	2.477	9.085	116	1.211
AVIA	.534	2.746	-.238	-1.281	.3830	1.797	15.277	116	1.683
BACA	.558	2.627	-.131	-0.643	.2114	2.315	7.165	116	0.795
BANA	.660	5.118	-.256	-2.069	.3393	2.400	12.810	116	0.999
BCH	-.180	-0.902	.203	1.062	.0877	2.653	3.212	116	0.459
CAMP	.058	0.232	-.004	-0.015	.1888	2.183	6.354	116	1.077
CANN	.453	1.830	-.370	-1.563	.1180	2.001	4.076	116	1.075
CARB	.145	1.102	-.042	-0.330	.4076	2.390	16.828	116	0.936
CELA	-.068	-0.629	-.066	-0.637	.5497	2.616	29.079	116	1.101
CENM	-.125	-0.901	-.054	-0.405	.2475	2.247	8.566	116	0.628
CERM	-.125	-0.838	-.222	-1.557	.4958	2.650	23.615	116	1.231
CRIS	.295	1.581	.019	0.105	.2646	2.424	9.277	116	1.475
DIAN	.410	1.095	-.078	-0.219	.0360	2.523	1.858	116	0.863
EATO	-.023	-0.119	-.105	-0.565	.3058	1.931	11.134	116	1.151
ECAT	-.006	-0.021	-.256	-0.953	.1217	2.058	4.187	116	1.138
FRIS	.190	0.984	-.059	-0.320	.2268	1.673	7.745	116	1.251
FUND	.099	0.468	-.025	-0.122	.0480	2.075	2.161	116	0.602

TABLE IV.36 (CONTINUED)

****

Ri	B4	T(B4)	B5	T(B5)	ADJ.R*2	D-W	F-STAT	T	S-W BETA*
GESA	.424	2.571	-.235	-1.485	.1865	2.463	6.273	116	1.020
IEM	.204	0.890	.333	1.516	.0983	2.261	3.507	116	1.120
INDE	.321	1.681	.142	0.777	.1523	2.408	5.131	116	0.963
KIMB	.106	0.646	-.251	-1.595	.3777	2.784	14.960	116	0.930
LAMO	.356	2.262	-.271	-1.803	.2163	2.494	7.348	116	0.857
LIVE	.110	0.920	-.069	-0.600	.1831	2.011	6.155	116	0.636
LORE	-.155	-0.663	.089	0.400	.1517	2.082	5.112	116	0.662
LUIS	.437	2.193	-.156	-0.818	.1362	2.231	4.628	116	0.896
MODE	.186	1.073	-.024	-0.146	.2877	1.850	10.292	116	1.177
MORE	.035	0.192	.072	0.419	.2341	2.018	8.030	116	1.112
NAFI	.081	0.733	-.109	-1.026	.2579	1.730	8.994	116	0.734
NEGR	-.089	-0.830	-.149	-1.459	.1760	2.412	5.913	116	0.451
PALA	.155	1.426	.126	1.217	.3338	2.221	12.525	116	0.968
PENO	.058	0.304	-.306	-1.674	.1731	2.282	5.815	116	0.616
SANB	.408	2.640	-.107	-0.723	.1854	1.955	6.236	116	0.592
SPIC	.129	0.997	-.319	-2.568	.4113	2.225	17.071	116	1.033
TAMS	.544	3.123	-.066	-0.397	.1494	2.137	5.041	116	1.000
TREM	-.049	-0.269	.260	1.502	.3049	2.596	11.088	116	1.544

****

TABLE IV.36 (CONTINUED)

* The Scholes and Williams is a consistent estimator of beta when shares are subject to infrequent trading. It is given by

$$b_i = \frac{(1+p_1+p_2)/(1+2p_1+2p_2)}{} B_1 + \frac{(1+2p_1+p_2)/(1+2p_1+2p_2)}{} B_2 + B_3 + \frac{(1+2p_1+p_2)/(1+2p_1+2p_2)}{} B_4 + \frac{(1+p_1+p_2)/(1+2p_1+2p_2)}{} B_5$$

where:

p_1 is the first order serial correlation coefficient for the market index.

p_2 is the second order serial correlation for the market index.

It is also a Dimson's corrected estimator. For more details see Fowler and Rorke (J.F.E. 1983).

TABLE IV.37

SCHOLES-WILLIAM BETA
PORTFOLIO OF MONTHLY RETURNS

$Rp = C + B1\ Rm(-2) + B2\ Rm(-1) + B3\ Rm + B4\ Rm(1) + B5\ Rm(2) + Ep$

****

Rp	C	T(C)	B1	T(B1)	B2	T(B2)	B3	T(B3)
Port. 1	.005	0.988	.069	0.879	.120	1.474	0.736	9.255
Port. 2	.007	1.346	-.072	-0.876	.045	0.535	0.840	10.101
Port. 3	.003	0.631	-.015	-0.181	.060	0.703	0.893	10.707
Port. 4	.007	1.288	-.077	-0.909	.092	1.042	0.938	10.867
Port. 5	.006	1.198	-.078	-1.009	.071	0.878	0.707	8.968

****

TABLE IV.37 (CONTINUED)

****

Rp	B4	T(B4)	B5	T(B5)	ADJ.R*2	D-W	F-STAT	T	S-W BETA*
Port. 1	.241	3.031	-.072	-0.943	.5667	2.396	31.085	116	1.065
Port. 2	.104	1.259	-.097	-1.214	.5295	2.162	26.889	116	0.850
Port. 3	.143	1.712	-.007	-0.089	.5812	2.520	32.915	116	1.062
Port. 4	.186	2.160	-.139	-1.679	.5881	2.556	33.840	116	1.030
Port. 5	.161	2.042	-.077	-1.017	.4963	2.641	23.664	116	0.802

****

* The Scholes and Williams is a consistent estimator of Beta when shares are subject to infrequent trading. It is given by

$$b_i = (1+p1+p2)/(1+2p1+2p2) \ B1 + (1+2p1+p2)/(1+2p1+2p2) \ B2 + B3 + (1+2p1+p2)/(1+2p1+2p2) \ B4 + (1+p1+p2)/(1+2p1+2p2) \ B5$$

where:

p1 is the first order serial correlation coefficient for the market index.
p2 is the second order serial correlation for the market index.
It is also a Dimson's corrected estimator. For more details see Fowler and
Rorke (J.F.E. 1983).

TABLE IV.38

SCHOLES-WILLIAMS BETA
INDIVIDUAL WEEKLY RETURNS

$$Ri = C + B1\ Rm(-2) + B2\ Rm(-1) + B3\ Rm + B4\ Rm(1) + B5\ Rm(2) + ei$$

****

Ri	C	T(C)	B1	T(B1)	B2	T(B2)	B3	T(B3)
ACCO	0.002	1.019	0.016	0.200	0.300	3.816	0.364	4.616
ACEY	0.001	0.276	0.074	0.717	0.089	0.868	0.728	7.061
ALUM	0.001	0.533	-0.041	-0.523	-0.016	-0.207	0.723	9.215
APAS	0.003	0.986	0.103	1.122	0.095	1.037	0.883	9.568
AVIA	0.003	1.027	-0.106	-1.028	-0.032	-0.313	1.348	13.053
BACA	-0.001	-0.257	0.069	0.679	0.081	0.795	0.732	7.173
BANA	0.002	0.973	0.083	1.013	0.057	0.693	0.625	7.586
BIME	0.000	0.026	0.173	1.033	0.046	0.276	0.560	3.333
CAMP	-0.003	-0.746	-0.149	-1.158	0.122	0.952	0.781	6.069
CANN	0.007	1.098	0.127	0.635	0.208	1.047	0.703	3.518
CARB	0.000	0.080	-0.052	-0.616	-0.019	-0.225	1.018	12.011
CELA	0.000	0.082	0.096	1.065	-0.147	-1.628	0.909	10.046
CENM	-0.001	-0.426	0.003	0.042	0.367	4.954	0.564	7.584
CERM	0.001	-0.623	0.078	1.068	-0.001	-0.013	0.988	13.536
CRIS	0.000	-0.040	0.146	1.722	-0.058	-0.683	0.822	9.661
EATO	0.002	0.817	0.093	0.975	0.048	0.506	0.913	9.559
ECAT	-0.002	-0.670	0.085	0.733	0.305	2.626	0.593	5.086
FRIS	0.001	0.464	0.168	1.842	0.238	2.620	0.977	10.716
FUND	-0.003	-0.694	-0.339	-2.690	-0.043	-0.344	1.197	9.475

TABLE IV.38 (CONTINUED)

Ri	C	T(C)	B1	T(B1)	B2	T(B2)	B3	T(B3)
GESA	-0.001	-0.365	0.123	1.876	0.175	2.675	0.406	6.199
IEM	0.000	0.123	-0.013	-0.112	0.085	0.761	0.381	3.406
INDE	0.004	1.908	-0.034	-0.482	0.111	1.569	0.440	6.226
KIMB	0.003	0.996	0.125	1.097	-0.054	-0.476	1.080	9.483
LAMO	0.003	1.373	0.062	1.003	0.164	2.644	0.176	2.834
LIVE	0.002	0.890	-0.090	-1.166	-0.078	-1.011	1.035	13.379
LORE	-0.000	-0.063	-0.035	-0.353	0.083	0.840	0.703	7.096
LUIS	0.005	1.544	0.087	0.793	0.339	3.097	0.977	8.884
NEGR	0.004	2.158	0.010	1.719	0.144	2.488	0.201	3.447
PALA	0.002	1.061	0.171	2.619	0.448	6.885	0.098	1.504
PENO	0.006	1.616	-0.190	-1.594	-0.108	-0.905	0.985	8.235
SANB	0.004	1.919	-0.085	-1.209	-0.074	-1.050	0.747	10.579
SPIC	0.003	1.514	0.134	1.929	0.156	2.250	0.610	8.772
TAMS	0.003	1.059	0.092	0.883	-0.048	-0.459	0.684	6.556
TREM	-0.000	-0.009	0.066	0.759	0.112	1.288	0.681	7.786

TABLE IV.38 (CONT.)

Ri	B4	T(B4)	B5	T(B5)	ADJ.R*2	D-W	F-STAT	T	S-W BETA*
ACCO	0.001	0.013	0.014	0.185	0.0598	2.12	7.56	517	0.666
ACEY	0.285	2.774	-0.078	-0.758	0.0996	2.30	12.41	517	1.068
ALUM	0.062	0.791	-0.007	-0.091	0.1366	2.31	17.33	517	0.722
APAS	0.061	0.661	0.109	1.190	0.1606	2.28	20.75	517	1.217
AVIA	0.144	1.398	0.028	0.269	0.2483	2.45	35.09	517	1.379
BACA	0.252	2.480	0.365	0.360	0.1014	2.13	12.65	517	1.132
BANA	0.067	0.814	0.114	1.396	0.1173	2.53	13.58	517	0.916
BIME	0.473	2.829	0.366	2.191	0.0449	1.81	5.85	517	1.519
CAMP	0.191	1.489	0.189	1.478	0.0727	2.13	9.08	517	1.104
CANN	0.264	1.325	0.132	0.663	0.0250	2.06	3.65	517	1.368
CARB	0.135	1.602	0.001	0.015	0.2186	2.52	29.87	517	1.078
CELA	0.336	3.727	-0.092	-1.026	0.1845	2.76	24.35	517	1.085
CENM	0.219	2.953	-0.101	-1.362	0.1515	2.02	19.42	517	1.013
CERM	0.101	1.393	0.163	2.248	0.2807	2.18	41.27	517	1.296
CRIS	0.102	1.200	0.175	2.064	0.1732	2.04	22.62	517	1.151
EATO	0.311	3.272	-0.116	-1.222	0.1666	2.20	21.63	517	1.221
ECAT	0.331	2.850	-0.154	-1.326	0.0732	1.94	9.15	517	1.113
FRIS	-0.115	-1.268	0.151	1.671	0.2084	2.02	28.17	517	1.377
FUND	0.093	0.741	0.053	0.421	0.1486	2.09	19.01	517	0.985
GESA	0.125	1.909	0.023	0.353	0.0960	2.02	11.96	517	0.811
IEM	0.051	0.457	0.235	2.118	0.0265	1.96	3.81	517	0.705
INDE	0.004	0.053	0.063	0.898	0.0705	1.96	8.83	517	0.571
KIMB	0.004	0.038	-0.109	-0.960	0.1475	2.57	18.85	517	1.049
LAMO	0.225	3.632	0.049	0.794	0.0549	1.99	7.00	517	0.632

TABLE IV.38 (CONT.)

****

Ri	B4	T(B4)	B5	T(B5)	ADJ.R*2	D-W	F-STAT	T	S-W BETA*
LIVE	-0.142	-1.845	0.020	0.258	0.2588	2.46	37.03	517	0.771
LORE	0.019	0.197	0.199	2.019	0.0952	2.05	11.86	517	0.944
LUIS	-0.191	-1.748	-0.069	-0.627	0.1471	2.18	18.79	517	1.129
NEGR	-0.032	-0.557	0.017	0.289	0.0346	2.18	4.70	517	0.409
PALA	0.190	2.925	-0.045	-0.690	0.1159	2.38	14.53	517	0.795
PENO	0.432	3.631	-0.168	-1.412	0.1310	2.24	16.55	517	0.960
SANB	0.018	0.251	-0.019	-0.269	0.1736	2.26	22.68	517	0.602
SPIC	0.132	1.906	0.000	0.002	0.1523	2.50	19.54	517	0.994
TAMS	0.186	1.790	0.284	2.738	0.0988	2.33	12.32	517	1.149
TREM	0.126	1.452	0.099	1.140	0.1157	2.20	14.50	517	1.048

****

* The Scholes and Williams is a consistent estimator of Beta when shares are subject to infrequent trading. It is given by

$$b_i = \frac{(1+p1+p2)}{(1+2p1+2p2)} B1 + \frac{(1+2p1+p2)}{(1+2p1+2p2)} B2 + B3 + \frac{(1+2p1+p2)}{(1+2p1+2p2)} B4 + \frac{(1+p1+p1)}{(1+2p1+2p2)} B5$$

where

p1 is the first order serial correlation coefficient for the market index.
p2 is the second order serial correlation for the market index.
It is also a Dimson's corrected estimator. For more details see Fowler and Rorke (J.F.E. 1983).

TABLE IV.39

SCHOLES-WILLIAMS BETA
PORTFOLIO OF WEEKLY RETURNS

$Rp = C + B1\ Rm(-2) + B2\ Rm(-1) + B3\ Rm + B4\ Rm(1) + B5\ Rm(2) + ep$

****
Rp	C	T(C)	B1	T(B1)	B2	T(B2)	B3	T(B3)
Port. 1	0.003	1.720	0.074	1.543	0.082	1.713	0.752	15.570
Port. 2	0.001	1.169	0.060	1.731	0.169	4.934	0.598	17.355
Port. 3	0.001	0.675	0.070	1.827	0.086	2.255	0.615	16.072
Port. 4	0.001	1.014	0.035	0.855	0.042	1.023	0.799	19.627
Port. 5	0.002	1.696	-0.065	-1.672	0.075	1.927	0.862	22.136
****

TABLE IV.39 (CONTINUED)

****

Rp	B4	T(B4)	B5	T(B5)	ADJ.R*2	D-W	F-STAT	T	S-W BETA*
Port. 1	0.063	1.315	0.131	2.719	0.3479	2.22	56.06	517	1.070
Port. 2	0.125	3.639	0.019	0.559	0.4135	2.20	73.77	517	0.938
Port. 3	0.210	5.498	0.010	2.624	0.3906	2.00	67.14	517	1.038
Port. 4	0.166	4.083	0.023	0.575	0.4481	2.25	84.80	517	1.041
Port. 5	0.083	2.135	-0.031	-0.791	0.4920	2.18	100.95	517	0.920

****

TABLE IV.40

A COMPARISON OF BETAS
WEEKLY RETURNS

****

Ri	S-W BETA (Rm +-2)	S-W BETA (Rm +-1)&&	MARKET-MODEL BETA	CAPM BETA
ACCO	0.666	0.689	0.369	0.371
ACEY	1.068	1.130	0.736	0.739
ALUM	0.722	0.759	0.714	0.712
APAS	1.217	1.081	0.902	0.900
AVIA	1.379	1.462	1.347	1.348
BACA	1.132	1.084	0.728	0.724
BANA	0.916	0.790	0.650	0.652
BIME	1.519	1.214	0.630	0.635
CAMP	1.104	1.128	0.804	0.805
CANN	1.368	1.253	0.737	0.737
CARB	1.078	1.131	1.008	1.006
CELA	1.085	1.104	0.907	0.908
CENM	1.013	1.187	0.569	0.573
CERM	1.296	1.155	1.036	1.037
CRIS	1.151	0.911	0.850	0.852
EATO	1.221	1.291	0.913	0.911
ECAT	1.113	1.253	0.592	0.593
FRIS	1.377	1.158	1.007	1.009
FUND	0.985	1.126	1.096	1.091
GESA	0.811	0.741	0.423	0.429
IEM	0.705	0.559	0.404	0.405

TABLE IV.40 (CONTINUED)

****

Ri	S-W BETA (Rm +-2)	S-W BETA (Rm +-1)&&	MARKET-MODEL BETA	CAPM BETA
INDE	0.571	0.588	0.460	0.464
KIMB	1.049	1.033	1.080	1.077
LAMO	0.632	0.617	0.199	0.206
LIVE	0.771	0.779	1.016	1.015
LORE	0.944	0.839	0.718	0.718
LUIS	1.129	1.139	0.979	0.981
NEGR	0.409	0.340	0.214	0.216
PALA	0.795	0.792	0.123	0.129
PENO	0.960	1.265	0.946	0.944
SANB	0.602	0.663	0.737	0.736
SPIC	0.994	0.945	0.627	0.629
TAMS	1.149	0.899	0.728	0.731
TREM	1.048	0.970	0.712	0.715

****

| AVG. | 0.99938 | 0.97279 | 0.73415 | 0.73524 |

****

TABLE IV.40 (CONT.)

****

Rp	S-W BETA (Rm +-2)	S-W BETA (Rm +-1)&&	MARKET-MODEL BETA	CAPM BETA
PORT 1	1.070	0.937	0.773	0.774
PORT 2	0.938	0.925	0.609	0.612
PORT 3	1.038	0.965	0.643	0.646
PORT 4	1.041	1.031	0.811	0.811
PORT 5	0.920	0.999	0.840	0.840

****

&& Scholes and Williams (J.F.E. 1977) have shown that for securities that do not miss an observation, the following gives a consistent estimate of beta;

$$bi = (Bi\text{-}1 + Bi0 + Bi\text{+}1) / (1 + 2p1)$$

where

Bi-1 is the parameter estimate obtained from the simple regression of Rit against Rmt-1.
Bi0 is obtained from the synchronous simple regression.
Bi+1 is obtained from the simple regression of Rit against Rmt+1.
p1 is the first order serial correlation for the market index.

TABLE IV.41

A COMPARISON OF BETAS
MONTHLY RETURNS

****

Ri	S-W BETA (Rm +-1)&&	S-W BETA (Rm+-2)	CAPM BETA	MARKET-MODEL BETA
ACEY	0.871	0.931	1.103$	1.135$
ALUM	0.619	0.589	0.659*	0.540*
APAS	1.279	1.211	1.074*	1.087@
AVIA	1.706	1.683	1.352	1.416
BACA	1.073	0.795	0.716	0.859
BANA	1.096	0.999	0.934*	0.851*
BCH	0.405	0.459	1.119@	0.543*
CAMP	1.267	1.077	1.089$	1.237$
CANN	1.084	1.075	0.869	0.818
CARB	0.941	0.936	0.996*	1.007*
CELA	1.112	1.101	0.614@	0.554@
CENM	0.702	0.628	0.910	0.786
CERM	1.233	1.231	1.232*	1.336*
CRIS	1.363	1.475	1.149*	1.141*
DIAN	1.038	0.863	1.019*	0.931*
EATO	1.207	1.151	1.089$	1.329$
ECAT	1.239	1.138	1.371$	0.800$
FRIS	1.253	1.251	1.124	1.061
FUND	0.654	0.602	0.700	0.633
GESA	1.025	1.020	0.925*	0.753*
IEM	0.994	1.120	0.631	0.499

TABLE IV.41 (CONTINUED)

Ri	S-W BETA (Rm +-1)&&	S-W BETA (Rm+-2)	CAPM BETA	MARKET-MODEL BETA
INDE	0.926	0.963	0.945	0.791
KIMB	1.063	0.930	1.073*	1.147*
LAMO	0.821	0.857	0.908*	1.315@
LIVE	0.655	0.636	0.777	0.572
LORE	0.783	0.662	0.925	0.951
LUIS	1.005	0.896	0.875	0.748
MODE	1.161	1.177	1.114	1.085$
MORE	1.145	1.112	0.946	0.970
NAFI	0.747	0.734	0.716	0.650
NEGR	0.489	0.451	0.534	0.348
PALA	0.990	0.968	0.783	0.623
PENO	0.832	0.616	0.938	0.870
SANB	0.687	0.592	0.705	0.624
SPIC	1.122	1.033	0.999	1.030$
TAMS	1.000	1.000	0.775	0.535
TREM	1.392	1.544	1.159*	1.184*

TABLE IV.41 (CONTINUED)

```
*************************************************************************
```

Rp	S-W BETA (Rm +-1)&&	S-W BETA (Rm+-2)	CAPM BETA	MARKET-MODEL BETA

```
*************************************************************************
```

PORT. 1	1.058	1.065	0.935*	0.910*
PORT. 2	0.906	0.850	0.883	0.854
PORT. 3	1.065	1.062	1.007*	0.996*
PORT. 4	1.114	1.030	0.981@	0.970@
PORT. 5	0.857	0.802	0.882*	0.797*

```
*************************************************************************
```

&& Scholes and Williams (J.F.E. 1977) have shown that for securities that do not miss an observation, the following gives a consistent estimate of beta:

bi = (Bi-1 + Bi0 + Bi+1) / (1 + 2p1)

where:

Bi-1 is the parameter estimate obtained from the simple regression of Rit against Rmt-1.
Bi0 is obtained from synchronous simple regression.
Bi+1 is obtained from the simple regression of Rit against Rmt+1.
p1 is the first order serial correlation for the market index.
$ Corrected for heteroscedasticity.
* Corrected for serial correlation.
@ Corrected for serial correlation and heteroscedasticity.

TABLE IV.42

CHOW TEST ON SCHOLES-WILLIAMS BETA
INDIVIDUAL WEEKLY RETURNS

Ri	S-W BETA OVERALL PERIOD 1972-1981	S-W BETA SUBPERIOD 1 1972-1976	S-W BETA SUBPERIOD 2 1977-1981	CHOW STATISTIC
ACCO	0.666	0.709	0.648	7.160*
ACEY	1.068	1.184	1.087	7.827*
ALUM	0.722	1.353	0.554	4.780*
APAS	1.217	1.000	1.252	6.978*
AVIA	1.379	1.644	1.349	6.223*
BACA	1.132	0.699	1.205	3.257*
BANA	0.916	0.806	0.940	0.529
BIME	1.519	1.493	1.474	53.890*
CAMP	1.104	1.184	1.083	20.941*
CANN	1.368	2.478	1.109	31.646*
CARB	1.078	1.478	0.962	12.456*
CELA	1.085	0.875	1.130	1.964
CENM	1.013	0.848	1.060	1.763
CERM	1.296	0.954	1.390	4.808*
CRIS	1.151	0.410	1.314	6.918*
EATO	1.221	1.175	1.194	2.907*
ECAT	1.113	0.769	1.185	7.003*
FRIS	1.377	0.851	1.523	9.515*
FUND	0.985	0.512	1.093	8.304*
GESA	0.811	0.949	0.781	1.270

TABLE IV.42 (CONTINUED)

****

Ri	S-W BETA OVERALL PERIOD 1972-1981	S-W BETA SUBPERIOD 1 1972-1976	S-W BETA SUBPERIOD 2 1977-1981	CHOW STATISTIC
IEM	0.705	1.369	0.524	9.390*
INDE	0.571	1.205	0.401	7.880*
KIMB	1.049	1.480	0.934	4.585*
LAMO	0.632	0.716	0.614	0.915
LIVE	0.771	0.891	0.762	1.809
LORE	0.944	0.232	1.125	15.567*
LUIS	1.129	1.476	1.014	29.231*
NEGR	0.409	0.659	0.328	2.082
PALA	0.795	0.610	0.841	0.987
PENO	0.960	1.055	0.900	32.008*
SANB	0.602	0.810	0.556	1.499
SPIC	0.994	1.205	0.916	4.138*
TAMS	1.149	0.792	1.177	9.882*
TREM	1.048	0.474	1.195	9.207*

****

* Significant at the 99% confidence level. That is, the Chow statistic is larger than the critical value of the F distribution with k and n1+n2-2k degrees of freedom and we can reject the null hypothesis that the parameters of the subperiod regressions are identical. The critical value of $F_{(6,515)}$ is 2.80.

TABLE IV.43

CHOW TEST ON SCHOLES-WILLIAMS BETA
PORTFOLIOS OF WEEKLY RETURNS

****

Rp	S-W BETA OVERALL PERIOD 1972-1981	S-W BETA SUBPERIOD 1 1972-1976	S-W BETA SUBPERIOD 2 1977-1981	CHOW STATISTIC
PORT 1	1.070	1.153	1.046	0.297
PORT 2	0.938	0.846	0.952	0.101
PORT 3	1.038	0.961	1.052	0.202
PORT 4	1.041	1.058	1.027	0.126
PORT 5	0.920	1.054	0.875	0.572

****

TABLE IV.44

TESTING THE EQUALITY OF THE INTERCEPTS

Ri = C + B1 Rm(-2) + B2 Rm(-1) + B3 Rm + B4 Rm(1) + B5 Rm(2) + B6 D* + ei

Ri	B6	T(B6)	S-W BETA	Ri	B6	T(B6)	S-W BETA
ACCO	0.004	0.924	0.680	FRIS	0.003	0.576	1.387
ACEY	0.008	1.294	1.092	FUND	-0.002	-0.319	0.978
ALUM	-0.001	-0.317	0.718	GESA	0.004	0.928	0.823
APAS	-0.009	-1.603	1.191	IEM	-0.003	-0.429	0.697
AVIA	0.005	0.778	1.393	INDE	0.001	0.326	0.575
BACA	-0.007	-1.121	1.113	KIMB	-0.001	-0.172	1.045
BANA	0.000	0.034	0.917	LAMO	0.000	0.116	0.634
BIME	-0.013	-1.352	1.481	LIVE	0.002	0.532	0.777
CAMP	0.001	0.210	1.109	LORE	-0.002	-0.297	0.939
CANN	-0.000	-0.028	1.368	LUIS	-0.000	-0.041	1.128
CARB	0.001	0.112	1.080	NEGR	-0.001	-0.429	0.405
CELA	-0.003	-0.514	1.078	PALA	0.003	0.677	0.804
CENM	0.000	0.092	1.015	PENO	-0.003	-0.413	0.952
CERM	-0.007	-0.158	1.294	SANB	-0.000	-0.070	0.601
CRIS	-0.006	-1.184	1.134	SPIC	-0.002	-0.430	0.990
EATO	-0.011	-1.966	1.189	TAMS	-0.010	-1.666	1.119
ECAT	-0.000	-0.018	1.113	TREM	-0.002	-0.418	1.042

TABLE IV.44 (CONTINUED)

****

Rp	B6	T(B6)	S-W BETA
PORT1	-0.003	-0.877	1.063
PORT2	-0.001	-0.428	0.936
PORT3	-0.002	-0.842	1.033
PORT4	-0.001	-0.558	1.037
PORT5	-0.000	-0.089	0.919

****

* D is a dummy variable that takes a value of 1 in the first subperiod (1972-1976) and a value of 0 in the second subperiod (1977-1981).

TABLE IV.45

SAMPLE AUTOCORRELATIONS FOR WEEKLY EXCESS RETURNS
ON 34 MEXICAN STOCKS FOR LAGS L=1,2,3,.....8
1972-1981

STOCK	1	2	3	4	5	6	7	8	T
ACCO	-.090*	-.009	.042	-.001	-.072	.009	.021	.015	521
ACEY	-.172*	.067	-.069	.081	-.029	.070	-.042	.049	521
ALUM	-.167*	-.091	.020	.009	-.032	-.037	-.035	-.006	521
APAS	-.140*	.090	-.124*	.049	-.068	-.030	.029	-.060	521
AVIA	-.226*	-.125*	.152*	-.092	-.024	.018	-.036	.022	521
BACA	-.083	-.002	-.091	.048	-.005	-.010	.005	.056	521
BANA	-.265*	-.081	-.138*	.156*	-.033	-.049	.029	.009	521
BIME	.083	-.047	-.065	-.044	-.037	.007	-.017	-.062	521
CAMP	-.060	-.080	-.064	.038	-.005	-.042	.025	.026	521
CANN	-.041	.015	.037	.005	.003	-.027	-.159*	.004	521
CARB	-.263*	-.081	-.002	-.054	.070	.006	-.039	.098	521
CELA	-.376*	-.151*	.246*	-.151*	.097	-.085	-.019	.106	521
CENM	-.136*	.011	-.004	-.033	-.086	.056	-.051	.062	521
CERM	-.079	-.038	-.020	-.101*	.016	-.097*	-.023	-.010	521
CRIS	-.003	.024	-.046	.020	-.094	.007	.055	.005	521
EATO	-.130*	.001	.001	.058	.027	-.007	-.088	.065	521
ECAT	-.031	.003	-.044	-.020	-.019	.019	.021	.094	521
FRIS	-.017	-.078	-.035	.118*	.073	-.007	-.094	-.024	521
FUND	-.036	-.115*	.036	-.002	-.055	.141*	-.030	-.034	521
GESA	-.036	-.048	-.029	.050	.070	-.037	.060	-.038	521
IEM	-.016	-.028	-.002	-.152*	-.045	-.088	.049	.067	521

TABLE IV.45 (CONTINUED)

STOCK	1	2	3	4	5	6	7	8	T
INDE	.012	-.056	-.054	-.036	.022	.004	.002	-.007	521
KIMB	-.289*	-.098*	.017	.046	-.009	.011	-.043	.035	521
LAMO	-.062	-.043	-.031	.017	-.043	-.014	.040	.048	521
LIVE	-.242*	-.024	.014	.080	-.073	.061	-.020	-.027	521
LORE	-.029	-.058	-.049	.006	-.009	-.105*	.025	-.015	521
LUIS	-.083	.036	-.045	-.015	-.008	-.034	-.055	.020	521
NEGR	-.094*	-.231*	.014	.016	.008	.043	-.011	-.031	521
PALA	-.268*	.011	.066	-.082	.087	-.086	-.042	-.054	521
PENO	-.133*	-.022	-.042	.065	.039	.021	-.017	.020	521
SANB	-.142*	-.026	.092	-.065	-.040	.008	.060	.038	521
SPIC	-.264*	.024	-.090	.128*	-.063	-.049	-.030	.076	521
TAMS	-.157*	-.013	-.035	.023	.047	-.003	-.080	-.032	521
TREM	-.109*	-.052	-.011	.002	-.007	.029	.152*	.009	521

* Sample autocorrelation is at least two standard errors to the left or to the right of its expected value under the hypothesis that the true autocorrelation is zero.

If the return series has been generated by a white noise, the sample autocorrelation coefficients for $L > 0$ are approximately distributed according to a normal distribution with mean zero and standard deviation $1/\text{sq.root of } T$. Thus, if a stock has 521 observations, one can assign a standard error of .044 to the first autocorrelation coefficient. Then, if the first autocorrelation coefficient was greater than .088, one would be 95% sure that the true autocorrelation coefficient is not zero.

TABLE IV.46

SAMPLE AUTOCORRELATIONS FOR WEEKLY EXCESS RETURNS
ON 34 MEXICAN STOCKS FOR LAGS L=1,2,3,.....8
1972-1976

STOCK	1	2	3	4	5	6	7	8	T
ACCO	.094	.044	.057	.037	-.166*	.040	.006	-.031	260
ACEY	-.122	-.034	-.035	.064	-.019	-.022	-.020	.024	260
ALUM	-.135*	-.128*	.098	-.043	-.144*	-.058	.006	-.063	260
APAS	-.189*	-.019	-.019	.053	.007	.071	.014	-.053	260
AVIA	-.198*	-.168*	.113	-.038	-.046	-.009	-.029	-.028	260
BACA	-.051	-.009	-.148*	-.037	.008	-.067	.102	.004	260
BANA	-.060	-.027	-.124	.041	.000	.031	-.056	.100	260
BIME	-.032	.048	-.072	.001	-.074	.105	.112	-.074	260
CAMP	-.021	-.135*	-.058	.024	-.013	-.023	.027	.061	260
CANN	-.018	.023	.027	.002	-.006	-.024	-.188*	-.011	260
CARB	-.153*	-.058	.032	-.073	.071	-.058	.044	.123	260
CELA	-.260*	-.063	-.048	-.049	.124	-.105	-.007	.034	260
CENM	-.076	-.132*	-.037	-.145*	-.068	.079	.016	.086	260
CERM	-.073	-.163*	.012	-.030	-.023	-.012	-.096	.093	260
CRIS	.021	.052	-.037	-.032	-.090	.076	-.008	.028	260
EATO	-.104	.062	-.018	-.059	.091	.135*	-.166*	.032	260
ECAT	.132*	.020	-.089	-.024	-.058	.052	.065	.105	260
FRIS	-.015	-.113	.120	.039	.057	.047	.044	-.002	260
FUND	-.195*	-.025	.050	.086	.056	.049	-.027	-.034	260
GESA	-.168*	-.015	-.006	-.017	.033	-.049	.005	-.008	260
IEM	.004	-.072	.011	-.121	-.064	.066	-.036	-.001	260

TABLE IV.46 (CONTINUED)

STOCK	1	2	3	4	5	6	7	8	T
INDE	.053	-.013	-.055	-.103	.028	-.024	.013	.055	260
KIMB	-.187*	-.093	.049	.120	-.065	-.024	-.102	-.034	260
LAMO	-.171*	.019	-.005	.054	-.026	-.003	.004	-.009	260
LIVE	-.374*	.035	-.030	.086	-.121	.119	-.029	-.018	260
LORE	.148*	-.120	-.116	-.029	-.009	-.054	.069	-.067	260
LUIS	-.112	.046	.093	-.090	.025	-.021	.040	.102	260
NEGR	-.035	-.285*	.002	.019	-.019	-.062	.047	.009	260
PALA	-.233*	-.076	-.005	.036	-.024	.019	.014	-.034	260
PENO	-.220*	-.045	-.066	.031	.005	-.001	-.091	.045	260
SANB	-.129*	-.146*	.216*	-.017	-.059	.047	.079	-.098	260
SPIC	-.164*	-.009	.004	-.001	-.011	-.062	.025	-.064	260
TAMS	-.249*	-.047	-.077	.152*	.019	-.022	-.031	-.005	260
TREM	-.140*	.039	-.033	.024	-.050	.008	.035	-.011	260

* Sample autocorrelation is at least two standard errors to the left or to the right of its expected value under the hypothesis that the true autocorrelation is zero.

If the return series has been generated by a white noise, the sample autocorrelation coefficients for L > 0 are approximately distributed according to a normal distribution with mean zero and standard deviation $1/\text{sq.root of } T$. Thus, if a stock has 260 observations, one can assign a standard error of .062 to the first autocorrelation coefficient. Then, if the first autocorrelation coefficient was greater than .124, one would be 95% sure that the true autocorrelation coefficient is not zero.

TABLE IV.47

SAMPLE AUTOCORRELATIONS FOR WEEKLY EXCESS RETURNS
ON 34 MEXICAN STOCKS FOR LAGS L=1,2,3,......8
1977-1981

****

STOCK	1	2	3	4	5	6	7	8	T
ACCO	-.193*	-.041	.031	-.024	-.022	-.011	.028	.038	261
ACEY	-.206*	.120	-.094	.088	-.037	.113	-.061	.061	261
ALUM	-.177*	-.072	-.031	.031	.030	-.028	-.061	.029	261
APAS	-.135*	.111	-.160*	.042	-.093	-.065	.022	-.064	261
AVIA	-.267*	-.070	.198*	-.169*	.007	.067	-.052	.084	261
BACA	-.096	.001	-.081	.068	-.012	.002	-.023	.064	261
BANA	-.294*	-.089	-.177*	.169*	-.035	-.064	.049	-.019	261
BIME	.119	-.079	-.068	-.050	-.032	-.036	-.071	-.064	261
CAMP	-.112	-.009	-.070	.055	.014	-.065	.023	-.011	261
CANN	-.181*	-.038	.101	.028	.066	-.052	.014	.113	261
CARB	-.329*	-.094	-.022	-.044	.068	.048	-.078	.076	261
CELA	-.395*	-.166*	.292*	-.167*	.093	-.085	-.020	.112	261
CENM	-.153*	.056	.005	.002	-.088	.049	-.074	.055	261
CERM	-.080	-.004	-.030	-.120	.029	-.123	-.005	-.037	261
CRIS	-.011	.014	-.052	.026	-.099	-.011	.063	-.009	261
EATO	-.161*	-.050	-.003	.119	-.022	-.096	-.063	.075	261
ECAT	-.171*	-.013	-.009	-.019	.011	-.014	-.011	.086	261
FRIS	-.018	-.065	-.096	.147*	.077	-.035	-.150*	-.039	261
FUND	-.014	-.129*	.032	-.014	-.071	.155*	-.030	-.031	261
GESA	.066	-.077	-.050	.099	.098	-.031	.100	-.059	261
IEM	.018	-.022	-.008	-.157*	-.043	-.113	.062	.077	261

TABLE IV.47 (CONTINUED)

****

STOCK	1	2	3	4	5	6	7	8	T
INDE	-.018	-.088	-.054	.012	.017	.024	-.005	-.054	261
KIMB	-.312*	-.099	.010	.029	.003	.020	-.028	.049	261
LAMO	.013	-.000	-.049	-.009	-.053	-.016	.053	.099	261
LIVE	-.174*	-.057	.036	.077	-.053	.032	-.018	-.031	261
LORE	-.057	-.048	-.039	.012	-.008	-.114	.016	-.007	261
LUIS	-.071	.032	-.100	.019	-.022	-.042	-.097	-.018	261
NEGR	-.121	-.206*	.019	.013	.019	.091	-.040	-.048	261
PALA	-.276*	.030	.081	-.109	.110	-.108	-.055	-.060	261
PENO	-.097	-.014	-.031	.076	.056	.026	.011	.008	261
SANB	-.149*	.029	.034	-.089	-.030	-.008	.044	.098	261
SPIC	-.297*	.037	-.122	.171*	-.078	-.047	-.050	.126	261
TAMS	-.141*	-.012	-.031	-.020	.046	-.007	-.102	-.031	261
TREM	-.098	-.086	-.003	-.007	.08	.034	.193*	.017	261

****

* Sample autocorrelation is at least two standard errors to the left or to the right of its expected value under the hypothesis that the true autocorrelation is zero.

If the return series has been generated by a white noise, the sample autocorrelation coefficients for $L > 0$ are approximately distributed according to a normal distribution with mean zero and standard deviation $1/\text{sq.root of } T$. Thus, if a stock has 261 observations, one can assign a standard error of .062 to the first autocorrelation coefficient. Then, if the first autocorrelation coefficient was greater than .124, one would be 95% sure that the true autocorrelation coefficient is not zero.

TABLE IV.48

SAMPLE AUTOCORRELATINS FOR WEEKLY EXCESS RETURNS
ON FIVE PORTFOLIOS FOR LAGS L=1,2,3,.....8
1972-1981

****

Portfolio	1	2	3	4	5	6	7	8	T
Port 1	-.104*	.003	-.026	.030	-.011	-.076	-.012	-.012	521
Port 2	-.203*	.069	-.011	.112*	.015	-.048	-.056	.061	521
Port 3	-.080	.007	-.039	.069	-.013	-.028	.060	.002	521
Port 4	-.157*	-.063	.060	-.032	.047	-.026	-.127*	.137*	521
Port 5	-.108*	.057	-.062	-.028	.037	.024	-.002	-.034	521

****

* Significant at the 95% confidence level.

TABLE IV.49

SAMPLE AUTOCORRELATIONS FOR WEEKLY EXCESS RETURNS
ON FIVE PORTFOLIOS FOR LAGS L=1,2,3,......8
1972-1976

****

Portfolio	1	2	3	4	5	6	7	8	T
Port 1	-.066	-.046	-.028	.044	-.043	-.072	-.093	.033	260
Port 2	-.202*	.103	.061	-.095	-.043	.008	-.030	.067	260
Port 3	-.157*	-.013	-.138*	.087	-.075	-.039	.097	-.032	260
Port 4	-.087	-.037	.043	.058	-.039	.052	-.029	-.031	260
Port 5	-.301*	.047	.007	.032	.055	-.090	-.042	.048	260

****

* Significant at the 95% confidence level.

TABLE IV.50

SAMPLE AUTOCORRELATIONS FOR WEEKLY EXCESS RETURNS
ON FIVE PORTFOLIOS FOR LAGS L=1,2,3,......8
1977-1981

****

Portfolio	1	2	3	4	5	6	7	8	T
Port 1	-.147*	.049	-.029	.010	.025	-.092	.065	-.061	261
Port 2	-.200*	.058	-.035	.163*	.040	-.066	-.063	.057	261
Port 3	-.050	.020	.005	.061	.005	-.031	.039	.015	261
Port 4	-.190*	-.076	.067	-.075	.085	-.062	-.171*	.208*	261
Port 5	-.048	.061	-.083	-.049	.030	.056	.013	-.053	261

****

* Significant at the 95% confidence level.

TABLE IV.51

SAMPLE AUTOCORRELATIONS FOR MONTHLY EXCESS
RETURNS ON 37 MEXICAN STOCKS FOR LAGS L=1,2,..8
1972-1981

STOCK	1	2	3	4	5	6	7	8	T
ACEY	-.074	.092	.047	.034	-.052	.028	.013	.081	120
ALUM	-.287*	-.058	.072	.065	.018	.048	.001	-.127	120
APAS	-.230*	-.025	.164	-.107	.155	-.008	.080	-.106	120
AVIA	.028	-.054	.215*	.010	-.022	.200*	.158	-.099	120
BACA	-.105	.184*	-.181	.034	-.092	.190*	-.012	.200	120
BANA	-.298*	-.045	.131	-.090	-.012	.098	-.052	-.022	120
BCH	-.315*	.367*	-.083	.148	.036	.160	-.048	.158	120
CAMP	-.111	-.113	-.071	-.044	.074	-.066	.073	-.148	120
CANN	-.053	.127	.000	.008	-.002	.126	.010	.095	120
CARB	-.201*	.189*	-.086	.019	.046	.017	-.059	.148	120
CELA	-.215*	.085	.093	-.060	.045	-.001	.178	.049	120
CENM	-.125	-.051	.139	-.267*	-.064	-.035	-.132	-.099	120
CERM	-.296*	.066	-.131	-.086	-.032	.016	.095	.045	120
CRIS	-.216*	.139	-.036	.009	.139	.009	-.051	.114	120
DIAN	-.276*	-.019	-.050	.002	-.022	-.008	.005	.027	120
EATO	.037	.013	.024	.157	.155	-.065	-.072	-.057	120
ECAT	-.047	.062	-.053	-.100	.024	.011	-.120	-.021	120
FRIS	.150	.081	.180	.207*	.042	.078	.024	-.066	120
FUND	.023	-.015	.006	-.050	-.136	.133	.072	-.059	120
GESA	-.288*	.091	.048	-.121	-.027	-.011	-.118	-.014	120
IEM	-.117	-.095	.234*	-.004	-.050	-.049	.074	.125	120

TABLE IV.51 (CONTINUED)

****

STOCK	1	2	3	4	5	6	7	8	T
INDE	-.184*	-.018	-.079	.225*	.085	-.065	-.164	.104	120
KIMB	-.360*	-.026	-.009	.021	.018	-.121	.114	-.013	120
LAMO	-.269*	.154	.013	-.075	.105	-.171	-.001	.013	120
LIVE	-.006	-.079	.096	-.176	-.026	.000	-.105	-.065	120
LORE	-.013	.039	-.012	-.196*	-.048	-.068	.166	.150	120
LUIS	-.151	.030	-.024	-.021	-.081	.008	-.127	.088	120
MODE	.072	-.141	-.044	.071	-.114	-.188	.036	.075	120
MORE	-.045	.133	-.030	.069	-.095	.106	-.107	-.044	120
NAFI	.124	.245*	.005	.048	-.017	-.146	-.024	-.095	120
NEGR	-.177	.019	-.114	.092	-.005	-.051	.033	-.017	120
PALA	-.240*	-.022	.001	.114	.055	-.079	-.025	-.056	120
PENO	-.147	.152	-.027	.159	.098	-.033	.082	-.090	120
SANB	.040	.086	.122	.015	.054	.056	.059	-.115	120
SPIC	-.087	-.081	-.119	-.004	.168	-.087	-.101	-.040	120
TAMS	-.121	.033	-.012	-.007	.029	.087	-.130	.181	120
TREM	-.235*	.163	.026	.103	.083	.014	.141	-.207*	120

****

* Sample autocorrelation is at least two standard errors to the left or to the right of its expected value under the hypothesis that the true autocorrelation is zero.

If the return series has been generated by a white noise, the sample autocorrelation coefficients for L > 0 are approximately distributed according to a normal distribution with mean zero and standard deviation 1/sq.root of T. Thus, if a stock has 120 observations, one can assign a standard error of .091 to the first autocorrelation coefficient. Then, if the first autocorrelation coefficient was greater than .182 one would be 95% sure that the true autocorrelation coefficient is not zero.

TABLE IV.52

SAMPLE AUTOCORRELATIONS FOR MONTHLY EXCESS
RETURNS ON 37 MEXICAN STOCKS FOR LAGS L=1,2,..8
1972-1976

STOCK	1	2	3	4	5	6	7	8	T
ACEY	-.125	-.025	.230	.009	-.066	-.044	-.020	.021	60
ALUM	-.294*	-.137	.062	.101	.008	.052	.025	-.133	60
APAS	-.087	.142	.084	-.071	-.130	.071	-.132	-.118	60
AVIA	.005	-.061	.220	.101	-.054	.138	.201	-.123	60
BACA	-.197	.105	-.296*	-.024	-.179	.210	.166	.091	60
BANA	-.172	.176	.182	-.022	-.033	.042	.011	-.014	60
BCH	.208	.066	.097	-.011	-.027	.087	.065	-.162	60
CAMP	-.108	-.160	-.132	-.029	.172	-.087	.089	-.147	60
CANN	-.081	.085	-.100	-.014	-.051	.161	-.095	.152	60
CARB	-.090	.242	-.108	.117	.051	-.013	-.038	.039	60
CELA	-.348*	-.072	.118	-.111	.223	-.287	.058	.142	60
CENM	-.235	.096	.024	-.197	.137	-.142	.080	.001	60
CERM	-.274*	.049	-.226	.045	-.119	.037	.048	.047	60
CRIS	-.324*	.127	-.237	.243	.022	.056	-.099	.019	60
DIAN	-.328*	.039	-.027	-.000	-.025	-.036	-.026	-.030	60
EATO	.108	-.030	-.001	.081	.146	-.153	-.048	-.079	60
ECAT	-.194	.145	-.105	.064	-.032	.082	-.063	.055	60
FRIS	.287*	.020	.211	.312*	.119	.085	-.030	-.005	60
FUND	.009	.040	.014	.007	.129	-.070	.092	.161	60
GESA	-.178	.061	-.150	.047	.051	-.242	.024	-.046	60
IEM	-.169	.063	-.247	.046	.070	-.042	-.010	.117	60

TABLE IV.52 (CONTINUED).

STOCK	1	2	3	4	5	6	7	8	T
INDE	-.114	-.008	.072	.064	.009	-.074	.019	-.157	60
KIMB	-.334*	-.027	.004	-.141	.210	-.190	.151	-.021	60
LAMO	-.217	.026	.172	-.269	.066	-.204	-.170	.123	60
LIVE	-.270*	-.182	.251	-.182	-.047	.099	-.054	.078	60
LORE	.154	-.152	.031	.154	.057	-.167	.092	.230	60
LUIS	-.169	.214	-.070	.027	-.165	.102	-.123	.035	60
MODE	.162	-.269*	-.182	.007	-.070	-.256	.020	.187	60
MORE	.105	.143	-.012	.121	.132	.067	.035	-.025	60
NAFI	-.087	.239	.040	-.023	-.124	.198	-.064	.184	60
NEGR	-.161	.026	-.047	-.110	.120	.003	-.048	.054	60
PALA	-.276*	-.111	.004	.134	-.007	.010	-.012	.073	60
PENO	-.416*	.091	-.150	.277	-.148	-.049	.051	-.016	60
SANB	-.094	.111	.341*	-.095	.117	.101	.086	-.027	60
SPIC	-.244	.063	.017	-.088	.239	-.316*	.091	.004	60
TAMS	-.082	-.091	.050	-.172	.129	-.028	.065	.111	60
TREM	-.232	.127	-.073	-.259	.093	.021	-.111	.023	60

* Sample autocorrelation is at least two standard errors to the left or to the right of its expected value under the hypothesis that the true autocorrelation is zero.

If the return series has been generated by a white noise, the sample autocorrelation coefficients for L > 0 are approximately distributed according to a normal distribution with mean zero and standard deviation 1/sq.root of T. Thus, if a stock has 60 observations, one can assign a standard error of .129 to the first autocorrelation coefficient. Then, if the first autocorrelation coefficient was greater than .258 one would be 95% sure that the true autocorrelation coefficient is not zero.

TABLE IV.53

SAMPLE AUTOCORRELATIONS FOR MONTHLY EXCESS
RETURNS ON 37 MEXICAN STOCKS FOR LAGS L=1,2,..8
1977-1981

STOCK	1	2	3	4	5	6	7	8	T
ACEY	-.080	.116	-.064	.041	-.088	.044	.024	-.158	60
ALUM	-.279*	.018	.084	.065	.012	-.053	.042	.099	60
APAS	-.289*	-.086	.139	-.164	.153	-.052	.076	-.122	60
AVIA	.048	-.149	.164	-.128	-.122	.159	.185	-.020	60
BACA	-.105	.185	-.183	.031	-.104	.166	-.064	.192	60
BANA	-.367*	-.162	.094	-.108	.005	.120	-.087	-.020	60
BCH	-.382*	.407*	-.098	.171	.009	.169	-.058	.228	60
CAMP	-.094	-.021	.084	-.032	-.135	-.037	.009	-.097	60
CANN	-.023	.184	.122	-.002	.061	-.023	.104	-.033	60
CARB	-.404*	.067	-.013	-.060	-.050	.057	-.099	.220	60
CELA	-.192	.125	.079	-.066	-.003	.059	.209	-.007	60
CENM	-.100	-.085	.163	-.278*	-.109	-.014	-.185	-.120	60
CERM	-.305*	.066	-.102	-.103	-.001	-.022	.140	.008	60
CRIS	-.196	.125	-.009	-.055	.129	.000	-.102	.100	60
DIAN	-.172	-.118	-.199	-.048	-.072	.039	.028	.132	60
EATO	-.082	-.056	-.068	.092	.142	-.064	-.131	-.194	60
ECAT	.111	-.037	-.010	-.171	.054	.054	-.115	-.149	60
FRIS	.069	.051	.139	.116	-.060	-.023	.087	-.069	60
FUND	.023	-.020	-.014	-.060	-.175	.109	.107	-.095	60
GESA	-.323*	.098	.101	-.173	-.046	.051	-.127	-.017	60
IEM	-.112	-.130	.317*	-.026	-.079	-.069	.078	.125	60

TABLE IV.53 (CONTINUED)

****

STOCK	1	2	3	4	5	6	7	8	T
INDE	-.244	-.049	-.193	.334*	.103	-.068	-.305	.212	60
KIMB	-.401*	-.029	-.025	.115	-.087	-.092	.083	-.030	60
LAMO	-.237	.286*	-.191	.134	.100	-.144	.087	-.228	60
LIVE	.181	-.027	.010	-.168	-.056	.037	-.111	.189	60
LORE	.030	.054	-.015	-.228	-.052	-.067	.180	.147	60
LUIS	-.140	-.136	.022	-.073	.017	-.115	-.064	.045	60
MODE	-.019	-.049	.009	.092	-.148	-.123	-.004	.022	60
MORE	-.089	.119	-.031	.025	-.163	.092	-.158	.014	60
NAFI	.182	.242	.009	.045	.016	-.260	-.023	-.169	60
NEGR	-.184	.015	-.133	.136	-.048	-.061	.056	-.074	60
PALA	-.236	.006	.001	.108	.072	-.097	-.025	-.091	60
PENO	.140	.194	.065	.032	.344	.019	-.037	-.012	60
SANB	.103	.064	.026	.087	.009	.011	.064	-.099	60
SPIC	-.004	-.150	-.197	.050	.145	.015	-.156	-.090	60
TAMS	-.157	.053	-.025	.035	.052	-.001	-.151	.199	60
TREM	-.241	.164	.053	.171	.087	.001	.190	-.269	60

****

* Sample autocorrelation is at least two standard errors to the left or to the right of its expected value under the hypothesis that the true autocorrelation is zero.

If the return series has been generated by a white noise, the sample autocorrelation coefficients for L > 0 are approximately distributed according to a normal distribution with mean zero and standard deviation 1/sq.root of T. Thus, if a stock has 60 observations, one can assign a standard error of .129 to the first autocorrelation coefficient. Then, if the first autocorrelation coefficient was greater than .258 one would be 95% sure that the true autocorrelation coefficient is not zero.

TABLE IV.54

SAMPLE AUTOCORRELATIONS ON MONTHLY PORTFOLIO
EXCESS RETURNS FOR LAGS L=1,2,...8
1972-1981

****

PORT	1	2	3	4	5	6	7	8	T
Port. 1	-.255*	.083	.016	-.056	.098	-.018	-.033	.102	120
Port. 2	-.128	.214*	-.137	.030	-.043	-.132	.054	.115	120
Port. 3	-.275*	.315*	-.077	.081	.044	.141	-.066	.041	120
Port. 4	-.289*	-.061	.073	.073	-.083	.005	.000	-.048	120
Port. 5	-.347*	-.058	.094	-.004	-.090	-.075	-.028	-.063	120

****

* Significant at the 95% confidence level.

TABLE IV.55

SAMPLE AUTOCORRELATIONS ON MONTHLY PORTFOLIO
EXCESS RETURNS FOR LAGS L=1,2,...8
1972-1976

****

PORT	1	2	3	4	5	6	7	8	T
Port. 1	-.341*	.040	-.151	.029	.035	.149	-.202	.198	60
Port. 2	-.210	.091	.066	.019	.185	-.278	.115	.030	60
Port. 3	-.335*	.169	.122	-.131	.200	-.079	.077	.057	60
Port. 4	-.380*	-.087	.038	.120	-.077	-.013	-.016	-.005	60
Port. 5	-.384*	-.114	-.027	.114	.013	-.107	-.031	.032	60

****

* Significant at the 95% confidence level.

TABLE IV.56

SAMPLE AUTOCORRELATIONS ON MONTHLY PORTFOLIO
EXCESS RETURNS FOR LAGS L=1,2,..8
1977-1981

****
| PORT | 1 | 2 | 3 | 4 | 5 | 6 | 7 | 8 | T |
****
|------|------|------|------|------|------|------|------|------|----|
Port. 1	-.217	.095	.096	-.126	.112	-.141	.035	.054	60
Port. 2	-.106	.254	-.224	.011	-.141	-.100	.087	.123	60
Port. 3	-.244	.367*	-.214	.244	-.070	.222	-.047	.003	60
Port. 4	-.122	-.011	.133	-.029	-.051	-.034	.115	-.110	60
Port. 5	-.299*	.003	.237	-.162	-.134	-.162	.076	-.138	60
****

* Significant at the 95% confidence level.

TABLE IV.57

TESTS FOR INDIVIDUAL SECURITIES
1/2 OF ONE PERCENT FILTER
(PERCENT PER WEEK)

	(1)	(2)	(3)	(4)	(5)
		STANDARD		X ADJUSTED FOR	(4) / (2)
		ERROR	NUMBER OF	TRANS. COSTS	TRANS.
					ADJUSTED
STOCK	X	X	TRANSACTIONS	(.35 OF 1%)	T
ACCO	0.3203	0.1186	116	0.2424	2.0432 @
ACEY	0.0942	0.1575	184	-0.0294	-0.1865
ALUM	-0.1038	0.1232	214	-0.2475	- 2.0083
APAS	0.1826	0.1468	182	0.0604	0.4112
AVIA	-0.0898	0.1736	204	-0.2269	-1.3068
BACA	0.2465	0.1576	190	0.1189	0.7542
BANA	0.0057	0.1274	226	-0.1461	-1.1471
BIME	-0.1140	0.2447	150	-0.2148	-0.8776
CAMP	0.2942	0.1975	194	0.1639	0.8298
CANN	-0.0421	0.2956	196	-0.1737	-0.5877
CARB	-0.1874	0.1398	222	-0.3366	-2.4082
CELA	-0.1080	0.1461	226	-0.2598	-1.7780
CENM	0.2424	0.1180	144	0.1456	1.2337
CERM	0.2205	0.1273	190	0.0929	0.7298
CRIS	0.1291	0.1362	158	0.0230	0.1686
EATO	0.1397	0.1527	210	-0.0014	-0.0091
ECAT	0.2177	0.1752	150	0.1170	0.6675

****

STOCK	(1) X	(2) STANDARD ERROR X	(3) NUMBER OF TRANSACTIONS	(4) X ADJUSTED FOR TRANS. COSTS (.35 OF 1%)	(5) (4)/(2) TRANS. ADJUSTED T
FRIS	0.0678	0.1491	178	-0.0518	-0.3473
FUND	-0.0732	0.2047	230	-0.2277	-1.1124
GESA	0.2353	0.1008	114	0.1587	1.5741
IEM	0.3923	0.1649	156	0.2875	1.7434
INDE	0.2815	0.1087	114	0.2049	1.8849
KIMB	0.1460	0.1790	196	0.0143	0.0798
LAMO	0.2229	0.0916	74	0.1732	1.8902
LIVE	-0.1500	0.1310	222	-0.2991	-2.2829
LORE	0.0148	0.1516	134	-0.0752	-0.4962
LUIS	0.0712	0.1725	192	-0.0578	-0.3350
NEGR	-0.0471	0.0849	140	-0.1412	-1.6630
PALA	0.2125	0.1008	140	0.1184	1.1748
PENO	-0.0710	0.1865	226	-0.2228	-1.1945
SANB	-0.1005	0.1140	202	-0.2362	-2.0721
SPIC	0.0614	0.1105	200	-0.0730	-0.6605
TAMS	-0.2041	0.1606	228	-0.3572	-2.2242
TREM	0.1620	0.1353	150	0.0612	0.4525
Port.	0.0785	0.0266		-0.0410	-1.2903

****

@ Positive and significant at the 95% confidence level.

TABLE IV.58

EFFECTS OF TRANSACTIONS COSTS ON THE PERFORMANCE
OF AN EQUALLY-WEIGHTED PORTFOLIO
1/2 OF ONE PERCENT FILTE

****

TRANSACTIONS COSTS %	PORTFOLIO X MEAN X_p	T-STATISTIC X_p	T-STATISTIC ADJUSTED FOR SAMPLE COVARIANCE X_p
0.00	0.07852	2.94481 @	2.46754 @
0.35	-0.04106	-1.53988	-1.29031
0.70	-0.16064	-6.02456	-5.04816
0.80	-0.19480	-7.30590	-6.12183
1.10	-0.29730	-11.14992	-9.34285

****

@ Positive and significant at the 95% confidence level.

TABLE IV.59

TESTS FOR INDIVIDUAL SECURITIES
ONE PERCENT FILTER
(PERCENT PER WEEK)

STOCK	(1) X	(2) STANDARD ERROR X	(3) NUMBER OF TRANSACTIONS	(4) X ADJUSTED FOR TRANS. COSTS (.35 OF 1%)	(5) (4)/(2) TRANS. ADJUSTED T
ACCO	0.3636	0.1186	98	0.2977	2.5106 @
ACEY	0.0635	0.1577	172	-0.0520	-0.3299
ALUM	-0.1265	0.1232	194	-0.2569	-2.0844
APAS	0.1931	0.1469	158	0.0869	0.5918
AVIA	-0.1782	0.1736	196	-0.3098	-1.7852
BACA	0.2619	0.1576	180	0.1410	0.8946
BANA	-0.0403	0.1273	186	-0.1652	-1.2978
BIME	-0.1132	0.2438	144	-0.2100	-0.8612
CAMP	0.2886	0.1975	192	0.1596	0.8078
CANN	-0.0276	0.2956	192	-0.1566	-0.5297
CARB	-0.1400	0.1398	202	-0.2757	-1.9712
CELA	-0.0951	0.1458	200	-0.2295	-1.5736
CENM	0.2408	0.1179	120	0.1602	1.3591
CERM	0.1965	0.1273	158	0.0903	0.7092
CRIS	0.2006	0.1353	132	0.1120	0.8276
EATO	0.1362	0.1526	196	0.0045	0.0294
ECAT	0.2678	0.1744	144	0.1711	0.9809

TABLE IV.59 (CONTINUED)

****

STOCK	(1) X	(2) STANDARD ERROR X	(3) NUMBER OF TRANSACTIONS	(4) X ADJUSTED FOR TRANS. COSTS (.35 OF 1%)	(5) (4) / (2) TRANS. ADJUSTED T
FRIS	0.0992	0.1491	156	-0.0056	-0.0375
FUND	-0.1453	0.2048	208	-0.2851	-1.3918
GESA	0.2674	0.1009	86	0.2097	2.0782 @
IEM	0.2789	0.1645	146	0.1809	1.0996
INDE	0.1929	0.1087	102	0.1244	1.1436
KIMB	0.0535	0.1783	176	-0.0647	-0.3629
LAMO	0.2226	0.0904	62	0.1809	2.0009 @
LIVE	-0.1720	0.1310	192	-0.3010	-2.2984
LORE	0.0034	0.1520	124	-0.0799	-0.5256
LUIS	0.1212	0.1725	170	0.0070	0.0408
NEGR	-0.0145	0.0849	114	-0.0911	-1.0727
PALA	0.2104	0.0996	116	0.1325	1.3304
PENO	-0.1277	0.1863	202	-0.2634	-1.4140

****

TABLE IV.59 (CONTINUED)

	(1)	(2)	(3)	(4)	(5)
		STANDARD		X ADJUSTED FOR	(4) / (2)
		ERROR	NUMBER OF	TRANS. COSTS	TRANS.
		X	TRANSACTIONS	(.35 OF 1%)	ADJUSTED T
STOCK	X				
SANB	-0.0764	0.1140	172	-0.1920	-1.6833
SPIC	0.0127	0.1103	176	-0.1056	-0.9567
TAMS	-0.2364	0.1606	208	-0.3761	-2.3423
TREM	0.0331	0.1349	140	-0.0610	-0.4518
Port.	0.0651	0.0266	-0.04184	-1.5709	

@ Positive and significant at the 95% confidence level.

TABLE IV.60

EFFECTS OF TRANSACTIONS COSTS ON THE PERFORMANCE
OF AN EQUALLY-WEIGHTED PORTFOLIO
ONE PERCENT FILTER

****

TRANSACTIONS COSTS %	PORTFOLIO X MEAN X_p	T-STATISTIC X_p	T-STATISTIC ADJUSTED FOR SAMPLE COVARIANCE X_p
0.00	0.06513	2.44572 @	2.04368 @
0.35	-0.04184	-1.57095	-1.31271
0.70	-0.14881	-5.58763	-4.66910
0.80	-0.17937	-6.73525	-5.62807
1.10	-0.27106	-10.17811	-8.50498

****

@ Positive and significant at the 95% confidence level.

TABLE IV.61

SUMMARY RESULTS FOR VARIOUS FILTER RULES

****

FILTER	T-STATISTIC ON Xp		PROFITABLE SECURITIES PER FILTER &
	BEFORE COMMISSIONS	AFTER .35% COMMISSION	
0.005	2.94481 @	-1.53988	1/34
0.010	2.44572 @	-1.57095	3/34
0.020	1.83625	-1.43587	2/34
0.030	0.89626	-1.85487	1/34
0.040	0.12620	-2.21894	1/34
0.050	-0.89186	-2.94404	1/34
0.100	-0.61455	-1.71460	1/34
0.150	-1.44464	-2.19193	2/34
0.200	-1.54779	-2.07381	2/34
0.250	-2.11552	-2.84682	1/34
0.300	-2.11655	-2.72067	1/34
0.350	-1.32856	-1.59941	1/34
0.400	-1.18823	-1.58352	1/34
0.450	-1.04830	-1.24352	0/34
0.500	-1.54600	-1.72449	0/34

****

@ The t-statistic on Xp is positive and significant at the 95% confidence level
& This is the number of profitable securities whose t-statistic on X is positive and significant after adjusting for transaction costs of .35%

TABLE IV.62

SUMMARY RESULTS FOR VARIOUS REVERSE FILTER RULES

****

| | T-STATISTIC ON Xp | | PROFITABLE SECURITIES |
REVERSE FILTER	BEFORE COMMISSIONS	AFTER .35% COMMISSION	PER FILTER &
0.005	-2.87608	-7.35486	0/34
0.010	-2.37300	-6.38185	0/34
0.020	-1.82950	-5.09326	0/34
0.030	-0.92461	-3.66853	0/34
0.040	-0.14400	-2.48212	0/34
0.050	0.88233	-1.16570	1/34
0.100	0.52550	-0.55972	0/34
0.150	1.19649	0.46519	2/34
0.200	1.52656	1.00235	2/34
0.250	2.14642 @	1.73256	3/34
0.300	1.90516	1.56905	4/34
0.350	0.65027	0.38884	1/34
0.400	0.40637	0.19188	1/34
0.450	-0.44119	-0.62093	0/34
0.500	0.18068	0.02180	2/34

****

@ The t-statistic on Xp is positive and significant at the 95% confidence level
& This is the number of profitable securities whose t-statistic on X is positive and significant after adjusting for transaction costs of .35%

TABLE IV.63

TESTS FOR INDIVIDUAL SECURITIES
TWENTY FIVE PERCENT REVERSE FILTER
(PERCENT PER WEEK)

	(1)	(2)	(3)	(4)	(5)
		STANDARD ERROR	NUMBER OF	X ADJUSTED FOR TRANS. COSTS	(4) / (2) TRANS. ADJUSTED
STOCK	X	X	TRANSACTIONS	(.35 OF 1%)	T
ACCO	-0.0700	0.1093	12	-0.0781	-0.7144
ACEY	-0.0800	0.1459	18	-0.0921	-0.6311
ALUM	-0.0414	0.1221	12	-0.0495	-0.4052
APAS	-0.0060	0.1415	14	-0.0154	-0.1085
AVIA	0.0790	0.1551	20	0.0655	0.4225
BACA	0.1555	0.1493	20	0.1421	0.9514
BANA	0.2229	0.1127	14	0.2135	1.8944
BIME	0.1269	0.2462	20	0.1135	0.4609
CAMP	0.1980	0.1904	26	0.1805	0.9479
CANN	0.5519	0.2661	20	0.5384	2.0235 @
CARB	-0.0153	0.1375	16	-0.0261	-0.1897
CELA	0.2547	0.1281	16	0.2439	1.9039
CENM	-0.0001	0.1164	14	-0.0094	-0.0807
CERM	-0.0137	0.1153	12	-0.0218	-0.1889
CRIS	-0.2045	0.1326	12	-0.2126	-1.6029
EATO	-0.2509	0.1488	16	-0.2617	-1.7585

TABLE IV.63 (CONTINUED)

****

| | (1) | (2) | (3) | (4) | (5) |
| | | STANDARD ERROR | NUMBER OF | X ADJUSTED FOR TRANS. COSTS | (4) / (2) TRANS. ADJUSTED |
STOCK	X	X	TRANSACTIONS	(.35 OF 1%)	T
ECAT	-0.0405	0.1762	20	-0.0540	-0.3062
FRIS	-0.4051	0.1490	10	-0.4118	-2.7630
FUND	0.3378	0.2049	28	0.3190	1.5572
GESA	-0.1150	0.0804	8	-0.1203	-1.4969
IEM	0.1963	0.1619	24	0.1802	1.1131
INDE	-0.0319	0.0907	10	-0.0386	-0.4253
KIMB	0.3911	0.1331	16	0.3803	2.8578 @
LAMO	-0.0279	0.0760	8	-0.0333	-0.4376
LIVE	0.0371	0.0872	10	0.0304	0.3481
LORE	0.0331	0.1428	14	0.0237	0.1659
LUIS	0.1581	0.1428	16	0.1473	1.0317
NEGR	0.0517	0.0439	4	0.0490	1.1151
PALA	0.0240	0.0840	12	0.0160	0.1904

TABLE IV.63 (CONTINUED)

****

	(1)	(2)	(3)	(4)	(5)
					(4) / (2)
		STANDARD		X ADJUSTED FOR	TRANS.
		ERROR	NUMBER OF	TRANS. COSTS	ADJUSTED
STOCK	X	X	TRANSACTIONS	(.35 OF 1%)	T
PENO	0.3727	0.1351	18	0.3606	2.6692 @
SANB	-0.0006	0.1039	12	-0.0087	-0.0837
SPIC	-0.1230	0.0900	6	-0.1270	-1.4115
TAMS	-0.0606	0.1479	16	-0.0713	-0.4820
TREM	0.0797	0.1337	18	0.0676	0.5052
Port.	0.0524	0.0244		0.0423	1.7325

****

@ Positive and significant at the 95% confidence level.

TABLE IV.64

EFFECTS OF TRANSACTIONS COSTS ON THE PERFORMANCE
OF AN EQUALLY-WEIGHTED PORTFOLIO
TWENTY FIVE PERCENT REVERSE FILTER

****

TRANSACTIONS COSTS %	PORTFOLIO X MEAN X_p	T-STATISTIC X_p	T-STATISTIC ADJUSTED FOR SAMPLE COVARIANCE X_p
0.00	0.05247	2.14642 @	1.60845
0.35	0.04235	1.73256	1.29832
0.70	0.03223	1.31870	0.98818
0.80	0.02934	1.20045	0.89958
1.10	0.02067	0.84571	0.63375

****

@ Positive and significant at the 95% confidence level.

CHAPTER V

CONCLUSIONS

The lack of liquidity in the secondary market (thin trading) for most of the stocks listed in the Mexican stock exchange seem to be the one of the main problems that professional investors face when they consider these securities as an investment alternative. This problem has not been reduced the way short selling procedures have been introduced but it can be completely eliminated with the implementation of specialists who stand ready to buy/sell at market prices when there are no sellers/buyers.

The fixed commission schedule set by the exchange and approved by the National Securities Commission is partially responsible for the high concentration of transactions among a very few brokerage houses. That is, an investor who wants to buy a listed stock will select that brokerage house which offers a better service in terms of advice, information and time of execution. This put small member firms and brokers at disadvantage.

Most of the distributions of individual weekly returns and portfolios are skewed to the right and are more peaked than normal distributions during the 1972-1981 period. The same kind of results are found using monthly returns on individual stocks and portfolios, although the significant coefficients are fewer and smaller. These tests along with the studentized range statistic reject the hypothesis that the samples come from a normal distribution in favor of the hypothesis that the samples come from a distribution that has fatter tails relative to a normal distribution.

Almost of the unsystematic risk is eliminated in the Mexican stock market by holding a portfolio of approximately 16-20 stocks. The rules given by the National Securities Commission concerning how common mutual funds must distribute their asset guarantee that the owners of such shares hold a well-diversified portfolio. An area for further research would be to investigate if other kinds of investors really hold well-diversified portfolios.

Over the 1972-1981 period, the average monthly mean and standard deviation of an equally weighted Mexican portfolio contaning 20 stocks is 0.023 and 0.069 respectively. The advantanges for a Mexican investors of an extended hedged diversification with U.S. stocks are substantial. The average monthly standard deviation of an equally weighted international portfolio contaning 20 stocks is reduced by .018 whereas its average mean is only 0.007 smaller.

The results of the serial correlation tets on on both weekly and monthly returns on individual shares as well as portfolios seem to indicate some linear dependencies in the period of time analyzed. Therefore, these tests indicate that the Mexican stock market was weak-form inefficient in the sense that the current prices did not reflect the sequence of past prices over the 1972-1981 period. There is a preponderance of negative serial correlation coefficients on the returns for individual stocks but not on the portfolio returns. The same kind of results are obtanied when autocorrelation tests are applied to monthly real returns. The fact that the inflation rate did not make a difference is understandable in the 1972-1981 period in which the change in the Consumer Price Index was never greater than 30 %. It may make a difference with a three-digit inflation or in any other period starting in 1982.

The Market Model or the C.A.P.M. beta of those stocks that are traded very infrequently in the Mexican stock market (less than 200 out of 521 trading days in the 1972-1981 period) is increased by nearly 90 % when estimation procedures that take into considerarion trading frequency are used. This is consistent with the analytical evidence and empirical evidence of Scholes and Willims (1977), Dimson (1979) and Fowler and Rorke (1983), showing that the betas of securities that trade less (more) frequently than the index used in their estimation are downward (upward) biased. However, the results are mixed when the betas of those stocks that trade very frequently (those with over 400 out of 521 trading days) are made.

The beta coefficients are unstable or non-stationary for individual shares but they are highly stable for portfolios. These results seem reasonable due to the fact that individual betas are modified over time in response to certain changes in the structure of corporations. This is one of the reasons why the theory of capital markets assume people hold well-diversified portfolios.

The results found on serial correlation tests on weekly and monthly returns are more pronounced on serial correlation tests on excess weekly and monthly returns, where excess return is defined here as the difference between actual return and what is expected under the C.A.P.M.. This significance is quite consistent over the 1972-1981 period for individual stocks but not for portfolios.

The overall results of applying both normal and reverse risk-adjusted filter rules developed by Sweeney (1986) on individual weekly prices show that only in very few cases the filters beat a buy-and-hold strategy after minimum transactions costs are taken into consideration. For an equally-weighted portfolio, significance before commissions is achieved in two out the 15 normal filters and in one out of the 15 reverse filters. However, all the significant profits are eliminated with the inclusion of minimum trasaction costs.

The main conclusion of this work is that the weak-form inefficiency found from serial correlation tests on both returns and excess returns may be statistically significant but of no economic importance once transactions costs are included into the analysis. There exists the possibilty that the weekly data is not able to capture the trends of the filters, in which case the negative serial correlation found on individual stocks may sill be of economic significance. This area for further research could be explored once daily data bases on securities prices have been developed.

BIBLIOGRAPHY

Alexander, S. S. "Price Movements in Speculative Markets: Trends or Random Walks." Industrial Management Review (May 1961): 7-26.

Alexander, S. S. "Price Movements in Speculative Markets: Trends or Random Walks, No. 2." Industrial Management Review (Spring 1964): 25-46.

Baesel J. B. "On the Assesment of Risk: Some Further Considerations." Journal of Finance (December 1974): 1491-1494.

Barnea A. and D. H. Downes. "Reexamination of Empirical Distribution of Stock Price Changes." Journal of American Statistical Association (June 1973): 348-350.

Beedles W. L. "On the Asymmetry of Market Returns." Journal of Financial and Quantitative Analysis (Sept. 1979): 653-660.

Beedles W. L. and M. A. Simkowitz. "A Note on Skewness and Data Errors." Journal of Finance (March 1978): 288-292.

Berglund T. and E. Liljeblom. "Market Serial Correlation on a Small Security Market: a Note." Journal of Finance (December 1988): 1265-1274.

Black F. M. Jensen and M. Scholes. "The Capital Asset Pricing Model: Some Empirical Results." In Studies in the Theory of Capital Markets. Edited by Michael Jensen. New York: Praeger. 1972.

Blume M. E. "The Assessment of Portfolio Performance: An Application to Portfolio Theory." Unpublshed PhD. Dissertation. University of Chicago. 1968.

-------- "On the Assessment of Risk." Journal of Finance (March 1971): 1-11.

--------"Betas and Their Regression Tendencies" Journal of Finance (June 1975): 785-796.

Bookstaber R. The Complete Investment Book: Trading Stocks, Bonds, and Options with Computer Applications. Scott, Foresman and Company.Glenview, Illinois. 1985.

Brealey, R. and S. Myers. Principles of Corporate Finance. McGraw-Hill. Third Edition. 1988.

Caso B. Jorge. El Mercado de Valores y la Banca: 40 Años de Historia. Documentos Mexicanos de Análisis. Instituto de Formación y Desarrollo de Operadora de Bolsa, S.A. México, 1986.

Cheng P. L. and M. K. Deets. "Portfolio Returns and the Random Walk Theory." Journal of Finance (1971): 11-30.

Clark, P. K. "A Subordinated Stochastic Process Model with Finite Variance for Speculative Prices." Econometrica (Jan. 1973): 135-155.

Cootner P. H. "Stock Prices: Random vs. Systematic Changes." Industrial Management Review (Spring 1962): 25-45. Also in Paul H. Cootner (ed.). The Random Character of Stock Market Prices. Cambridge: M.I.T. Press. 1964. pp. 231-52.

David H. A.; H. O. Hartley and E. S. Pearson. "The Distribution of the Ratio, in a Single Normal Sample, of Range to Standard Deviation." Biometrika (1954): 482-493.

Der-Ann H.; R. Miller and D. Wichern. "On the Stable Paretian Behavior of Market Prices." Journal of the American Statistical Association (March 1974): 108-13.

Dimson E. "Risk Measurement When Shares are Subject to Infrequent Trading." Journal of Financial Economics (June 1979): 197-226.

Dryden M. M. "A Source of Bias in Filter Tests of Share Prices." Journal of Business (Jan. 1969): 321-325.

Elton E. J. and M. J. Gruber. Modern Portfolio Theory and Investment Analysis. Second Edition. John Wiley and Sons Inc. 1984.

Evans J. L. and S. H. Archer. "Diversification and the Reduction of Dispersion: An Empirical Analysis." Journal of Finance (December 1968): 761-67.

Fama E. F. "The Behavior of Stock Market Prices." Journal of Business (January 1965): 34-105.

-------- "Portfolio Analysis in a Stable Paretian Market." Management Science (January 1965): 404-418.

-------- "Risk, Return and Equilibrium: Some Clarifying Comments." Journal of Business (March 1968): 409-419.

-------- "Risk, Return and Equilibrium." Journal of Political Economy (January-February 1971): 30-55.

-------- "Efficient Capital Markets: A Review of Theory and Empirical Work." Journal of Finance (May 1970): 383-417. Reprinted in James Lorie and Richard Brealey, ed. Modern Developments in Investment Management: A Book of Reading. Second Edition. Hinsdale Ill. Dryden Press. 1978. pp. 109-153.

-------- Foundations of Finance. Basic Books. 1976.

Fama E. F. and M. E. Blume. "Filter Rules and Stock Market Trading." Journal of Business (January 1966): 226-41.

Fama E. F. and J. D. MacBeth. "Risk, Return, and Equilibrium: Empirical Tests." Journal of Political Economy (May-June 1973): 607-36.

Fama E. F. and R. Roll. "Some Properties of Symmetric Stable Distributions." Journal of American Statistical Association (September 1968): 817-836.

-------- "Parameter Estimates for Symmetric Stable Distributions." Journal of American Statistical Association (June 1971): 331-338.

Fisher L. "Some New Stock-Market Indexes." Journal of Business (January 1966): 191-225.

Fisher L. and J. Lorie. "Some Studies of Variability Returns on Investments in Common Stocks." Journal of Business (April 1970): 99-134. Reprinted in James Lorie and Richard Brealy ed. Modern Developments in Investment Management: A Book of Readings. Second Edition. Hinsdale Ill. Dryden Press. 1978. pp. 43-77.

Fowler D. J. and C. H. Rorke. "Risk Measurements When Shares are Subject to Infrequent Trading." Journal of Financial Economics (August 1983): 279-283.

Fowler D. J.; C. H. Rorke and V. M. Jog. "Heteroscedasticity, R2 and Thin Trading on the Toronto Stock Exchange." Journal of Finance (Dec. 1979): 1201-1210.

Glejer H. "A New Test for Heteroscedasticity." Journal of the American Statistical Association (Vol. 64, 1969): 316-323.

Harris L. "Cross-Security Tests of the Mixture of Distributions Hypothesis." Journal of Financial and Quantitative Analysis (March 1986): 39-46.

-------- "Transaction Data Tests of the Mixture of Distribution Hypothesis." Journal of Financial and Quantitative Analysis (June 1987): 127-141.

Harvey C. R. "The World Price of Covariance Risk." Journal of Finance (March 1991): 111-157.

Hawawini G. A. "An Analytical Examination of the Intervaling Effect on Skewness and other Moments." Journal of Financial and Quantitative Analysis (Dec. 1980): 1121-1127.

Heyman T. Inversión Contra Inflación. Editorial Milenio. Tercera Edición. México. 1988.

Jegadeesh N. "Evidence of Predictable Behavior of Security Returns." Journal of Finance (July 1990): 881-898.

Kendall M. G. "The Analysis of Economic Time Series, Part I." Journal of the Royal Statistical Society (1953): 11-25.

King B. F. "Market and Industry Factors in Stock Price Behavior." Journal of Business (January 1966): 139-190.

Kon S. J. "Models of Stock Returns: A Comparison." Journal of Finance (March 1984): 147-164.

Levy R. A. "Relative Strenght as Criterion for Investments Selection." Journal of Finance (Dec. 1967): 595-610.

-------- "Stationarity of Beta Coefficients." Financial Analysts Journal (November-December 1971): 55-63.

Lessard D. "International Portfolio Diversification: A Multivariate Analysis for a Group of Latin American Countries." Journal of Finance (June 1973): 619-633.

Levy H. and M. Sarnat. "International Diversification of Investments Portfolios." American Economic Review (September 1970)" 668-675.

Linter J. "The Valuation of Risky Assets and the Selection of Risky Investments in Stock Portfolios and Capital Budgets." Review of Economics and Statistics (February 1965): 13-37.

-------- "Security Prices, Risk and Maximal Gain from Diversification." Journal of Finance (December 1965): 587-615.

Logue D. E. and R. J. Sweeney. ":White Noise" in Imperfect Markets" The Case of the Franc/Dollar Exchange Rate." Journal of Finance (June 1977): 761-68.

Mandelbrot B. "The Variation of Certain Speculatives Prices." Journal of Business (October 1963): 394-419.

-------- "Forecasts of Future Prices, Unbiased Markets, and Martingale Models." Journal of Business (January 1966) Supplement.

Markowitz H. M. Portfolio Selection: Efficient Diversification of Portfolios. New York. John Wiley and Sons Inc. 1959.

-------- "Foundations of Portfolio Theory". Journal of Finance (June 1991): 469-477.

McQueen G. and S. Thorley. "Are Stocks Returns Predictable? A Test Using Markov Chains." Journal of Finance (March 1991): 239-263.

Morgan I. G. "Stock Prices and Heteroskedasticity." Journal of Business (Oct. 1976): 496-508.

Mossin J. "Equilibrium in a Capital Asset Market." Econometrica (October 1966): 768-783.

Officer R. R. "A Time Series Examination of the Market Factor of the New York Stock Exchange." PhD. Dissertation. University of Chicago. 1971.

Osborne M. F. M. "Brownian Motion in the Stock Market." Operation Research (March-April 1959): 145-73.

Ortiz E. "Caminata al Azar en México: Importancia y Evidencia de la Bolsa Mexicana de Valores." Contaduría y Administración (Nos. 104-105, 1980): 65-109.

Perry P. R. "Portfolio Serial Correlation and Nonsynchronous Trading." Journal of Financial and Quantitative Analysis (Dec. 1985): 517-23.

Pogue G. A. and B. H. Solnik. "The Market Model Applied to European Common Stocks": Some Empirical Results." Journal of Financial and Quantitative Analysis (December 1974): 917-944.

Praetz P. D. "Rates of Return on Filter Tests." Journal of Finance (March 1976): 71-75.

-------- "A General Test of Filter Effect." Journal of Financial and Quantitative Analysis (June 1979): 385-394.

Roberts H. V. "Statistical Versus Clinical Prediction of the Stock Market." Unpublish paper presented to the Seminar on the Analysis of Security Prices. University of Chicago. May 1967.

-------- "Stock Market Patterns and Financial Analysis." Journal of Finance (March 1959): 1-10. Reprinted in James Lorie and Richard Brealey, ed. Modern Developments in Investment Management: A Book of Readings. Second Edition. Hindsdale Ill. Dryden Press. 1978. pp. 154-163.

Roll R. "R2" Journal of Finance. (July 1988): 541-566.

Scholes M. J. and J. Williams. "Estimating Betas from Nonsynchronous Data." Journal of Financial Economics (December 1977): 309-328.

Schwert G. W. "Why Does Stock Market Volatility Change Over Time?" Journal of Finance (December 1989): 1115-1153.

Schwert G. W. and Paul J. Seguin. "Heteroskedasticity in Stock Returns." Journal of Finance (September 1990)" 1129-1155.

Sharpe W. F. "A Simplified Model for Portfolio Analysis." Management Science (January 1962): 277-293.

-------- "Capital Asset Prices: A Theory of Market Equilibrium Under Conditions of Risk." Journal of Finance (September 1964): 425-42.

-------- "Capital Asset Prices With and Without Negative Holdings." Journal of Finance (June 1991): 489-509.

Singleton J. C. and J. Wingender. "Skewness Persistence in Common Stock Returns. Journal of Financial and Quantitative Analysis (Sept. 1986): 335-341.

Solnick B. "Why not Diversify Internationally?." Financial Analysts Journal (July-Aug. 1974): 48-53.

-------- "The Distribution of Daily Stock Returns and Settlement Procedures: The Paris Bourse." Journal of Finance (December 1990): 1601-1609.

Statman M. "How many Stocks Make a Diversified Portfolio?." Journal of Financial and Quantitative Analysis (September 1987): 353-363.

Sweeney R. J. "Some New Filter Rule Tests: Methodology and Results." Mimeo. Claremont Mckenna College and Claremont Graduate School. 1986.

Tauchen G. and M. Pitts. "The Price Variability-Volume Relationship on Speculative Markets." Econometrica (March 1983): 485-505.

Tobin J. "On the Efficiency of the Financial System." Lloyd's Bank Review (July 1984): 1-15.

Wagner W. H. and S. C. Lau. "The Effect of Diversification on Risk." Financial Analysts Journal (November-December 1971): 48-53.

Working H. "Note on the Correlation of First Differences of Averages in a Random Chain." Econometrica (Vol. 28, 1960): 916-918.